Get Started in Jazz

Rodney Dale

Rodney Dale is an author, editor and publisher, and a co-founder of Cambridge Consultants Ltd, the UK's first independent research and development organization. He has been involved with jazz for over 40 years, including playing piano with a number of bands, and organizing classes and workshops on jazz appreciation. He has written some 60 books, principally on non-fiction topics including technology, computing and jazz.

To my dear wife, Judith, for her ever-ready help and support

Teach Yourself ®

Get Started in Jazz

Rodney Dale

First published in Great Britain in 2004 by Hodder & Stoughton. An Hachette UK company.

First published in US in 2004 by The McGraw-Hill Companies, Inc.

This edition published 2014

British Library Cataloguing in Publication Data: a catalogue record for this title is available from the British Library.

Library of Congress Catalog Card Number: on file.

10 9 8 7 6 5 4 3 2 1

Cover image © Furtseff / Shutterstock

Typeset by Cenveo® Publisher Services.

Printed and bound in Great Britain by CPI Group (UK) Ltd., Croydon, CRO 4YY.

Hodder & Stoughton policy is to use papers that are natural, renewable and recyclable products and made from wood grown in sustainable forests. The logging and manufacturing processes are expected to conform to the environmental regulations of the country of origin.

Hodder & Stoughton Ltd

338 Euston Road

London NW1 3BH

www.hodder.co.uk

Contents

Acknowledgements   vii

Preface   viii

Introduction   1

Part 1 The history and development of jazz

1   What is jazz?   7

2   The three elements of music   11

3   The raw materials of jazz   15

4   The birth of jazz   19

5   Pioneers of jazz   23

6   The blues   33

7   Piano ragtime and stride   41

8   New Orleans jazz migrates   47

9   Big bands   51

10   Boogie-woogie   57

11   The swing era   61

12   Bop and afterbop   67

13   New Orleans revival   77

Part 2 The structure of jazz

14   The instruments of jazz   85

15   Rudiments of music   95

16   Practical music making   101

17   Scales and chords   105

18   Further chords   115

19   Chord sequences   123

Notes to accompany the recording   133

Index   135

Acknowledgements

For their help and advice in the early stages of the development of this text, I am most grateful to Pat Brandon, Susanne and Alastair Lyle, Peter Rayner, Elizabeth Stead, Ken Vail and Rebecca Weaver.

For this updated edition, Owen Bryce made a number of helpful observations on the original text, all of which have enhanced this version. Charlotte Edwards began the updating and Lyndsey Goddard carried it forward intensively. This edition is considerably enhanced by the inclusion of a recording, and I am particularly grateful to that doyen of early jazz styles, Keith Nichols, for the interest he has taken in the project and for the pieces he has written specially to illustrate the development of jazz.

I am very grateful to all for their help but, in the time-honoured way, I take sole responsibility for any errors of fact or of taste that have slipped through.

Preface

Most authors never explain the point of view from which they write. Trying to work out the author's stance may add to the reader's fun – or infuriation – but is unhelpful in a Teach Yourself text. Here, surely, the author owes it to you to reveal his or her biases at the start.

My definition of jazz is: 'The syncopated, often improvised, music that arose primarily in, and spread from, New Orleans in the first quarter of the twentieth century.' Although, like most people with strongly held views, I have become more benign with age, I have yet to come to a full appreciation of the more extreme forms of modern jazz. However, the more acceptable and respected jazz becomes and the more it is taught as an academic subject, the further it travels from its roots – and the less its modern practitioners know about its roots, the less it owes to those roots. So this book is concerned with *roots* – the beginnings of the music – and concentrates on jazz up to World War II (about which there's plenty to say), although I will tell you about bop and the New Orleans revival, with particular reference to jazz in Britain. This book is for anyone who, for whatever reason, wants to start at the beginning and learn about, or be reminded of, exactly where the music came from.

I became interested in jazz through our acoustic gramophone at an early age and started to play the piano by ear in my mid-teens with a number of like-minded school friends who were, fortunately, interested in other instruments. I have never got on particularly well with sight-reading dots, but I do know how they work. I also understand the difficulty many dot readers have with chords and certainly vice versa. My knowledge of chords progressed rapidly when the trumpeter Joe Lyde gave me a chord book so that I could play in his band in the old Masonic Hall in Cambridge in 1955. Thence to the New Orleans Jassmen with the late Dud Clews (cornet), Chris Cook (clarinet), Roy Rubinstein (trombone) and Nick Dyer (drums). I went on to play with many local traditional, or Dixieland, groups. Since we often supported nationally or internationally known bands, I have heard a great deal of live jazz in my time and I hope that you will get as much pleasure from the music as I have over the years.

I should say a word about political correctness. I can see no point in revisionism – rewriting the facts for the benefit of those who have been conditioned to feel squeamish about such things. 'Minstrel shows' and 'coon songs' were popular American entertainments a century ago. Early jazz was played almost exclusively by males and, when it became a general entertainment, was generally sung by 'girl singers'. Early blues were sung by black males, and 'two-timin' women' were a recurrent theme. That's the way it was and I hope that that glimpse of a culture of the past will enhance rather than detract from your present enjoyment.

I have lightened the text with a few anecdotes and wry comments. This approach may encourage you to contact me; if you do, I will endeavour to reply (please send an SAE if writing by post) and will certainly take heed of what you say for future editions.

Rodney Dale
Haddenham, Cambridgeshire
info@fernhouse.com

Introduction

The scope of this book

This book is not primarily a music tutor in that it doesn't set out to teach you how to play any particular instrument. However, it is necessary, in my view, to have at least a basic knowledge of how the music is constructed if you are to gain any understanding of it, in much the same way as someone who understands what goes on under the bonnet of a car should be a better driver. So if you do play or have access to an instrument – particularly a keyboard – and wish to try playing jazz, you will find some guidance in these pages.

One of the problems inherent in presenting any multidimensional subject – and history is nothing if not multidimensional – is how to discuss it in a linear way. Books have a habit of starting with Chapter 1, followed by Chapter 2, and so on, while most topics comprise several strands developing simultaneously. Jazz is certainly no exception to that, so while you're reading about any particular topic, you must remember the other things that were going on in the world at the same time and try to relate the various strands as you find out what they all are.

I have divided the text into two parts:

Part one: the history and development of jazz, including profiles of players and bands, and

Part two: the structure of jazz.

PART ONE: HISTORY AND DEVELOPMENT
We start by looking at what jazz is – and isn't – so that we'll know it when we meet it. Then we look at the background to jazz – the three elements of music (rhythm, melody and harmony) and the musical strands that came together to provide the environment from which jazz emerged. We continue this history by looking at what happened to jazz after it emerged – where it spread to and what it developed into. I have provided some information on key musicians and bands to accompany each topic.

PART TWO: STRUCTURE
We begin with a survey of the range of (western) musical instruments normally used in jazz. This gives some information about how the instruments work and how they are used in bands. If it inspires you to become a player, so much the better.

Then you will find a fairly detailed exposition of the musical structure of jazz; it will enhance your understanding of the music and may give you even *more* encouragement to become a player.

Summary

To summarize, this book:

▶ defines jazz by looking at its origins and development

▶ gives short biographies of important players and bands in various styles and periods

▶ describes the instruments and musical structure of jazz

▶ gives a number of pointers for you to develop your interest in jazz.

My purpose is to help you to:

▶ choose to whom and what to listen

- improve your understanding of the background to and structure of what you hear

- relate what you hear to the instruments on which it is played (and, if you are an instrumentalist, to understand better how to go about *playing* jazz).

You can use *Teach Yourself Jazz* in several ways, among them:

- reading it from cover to cover

- dipping into it to find specific information

- as a manual to help you to listen to – and even play – jazz.

The recording

The recording – available as a CD with the physical book and as an enhanced feature of the ebook – is in two parts. In Part 1, Keith Nichols illustrates the development of jazz, as described in Part one of the text. You should listen to Part 2 of the CD while reading the examples and exercises in Part two of the text. There is more information about the CD at the back of the book and on the disk itself.

Throughout the book, this symbol indicates that the relevant section is to be found on the recording.

Track 1

Beyond this book

LISTENING

Most people learn to talk and sing by listening to others and practising their developing skills. If you take up a foreign language you can get only so far with a book – you have to *listen* to find out how to pronounce words and how to vary your voice and practise how to 'speak like a native'.

Finding out about jazz is similar to taking up a new language. You can read about it on the page, but you must listen to as much of it as you can – on recordings, on the radio and TV (watch out for films featuring jazz) and live. The inclusion of the recorded examples related to the text is a great step forward in Teach Yourself presentation, but don't forget: if the opportunity arises and you have some basic ability, try playing jazz; there's no better way of getting to its heart.

RECORDINGS

There is so much jazz available on CD or for digital download today that it would be a work of supererogation if I were to try to provide listening lists rather than to recommend those 1,700 pages of *The Penguin Guide to Jazz Recordings* by Richard Cook and Brian Morton, which reached its ninth edition in 2008 (Richard Cook sadly died in 2007). 'The comprehensive critical guide to recorded jazz from its beginnings until the present.'

As to whom to listen to, I have provided some potted biographies of important musicians and bands in Part one and a lengthy list of musicians in an appendix. I apologize to any aficionado whose own choices might be different from mine, but we have to start somewhere. The information will help you to make a start with compiling your own listening list.

There are, of course, still countless 78s, LPs and EPs in circulation and there is a lot of excitement to be had in finding some rare gem in a second-hand shop or at a jumble sale. Moreover, there is still an enormous amount of older material not yet transferred to CD or other digital format and a great deal of it never will be as long as there are adverse commercial pressures. So keep your old record player in working order (I've just seen a modern version of an old record player in one of those unstoppable catalogues, which might be the very thing you've been looking for) and keep hunting.

FURTHER READING

I suggest that you first familiarize yourself with the basics of jazz from this book and then decide what or whom you want to read more about. There is an ever-growing jazz bibliography and, now that most libraries and bookshops have continually updated online catalogues, finding a book – or a record – on a subject should be easier than it was – and don't forget the Internet, where many musicians have fan club websites and whence you may also seek used books and recordings.

One book that you will find helpful with its breadth of information is *Jazz Milestones* compiled by Ken Vail, published by Sanctuary (now out of print but available second-hand). Here you will find laid out year by year (1900–1990) a chronicle of events, births, deaths, compositions, books, films, recordings and dozens of evocative photographs. It will help you to see who did what when and what other people were doing at the same time. It will help you plan your visits to book and record shops and help you to sniff out jazz films – which often provide invaluable contemporary atmosphere, even if the content needs taking with a pinch of salt. I commend to you also the four books *Let's Play Jazz* by Owen Bryce.

Part 1

The history and development of jazz

What is jazz?

In this chapter you will learn:

- ▶ *some definitions of jazz*
- ▶ *the difference between jazz and other music*
- ▶ *about jazz and the six senses*
- ▶ *about some earlier views of jazz.*

Many books about jazz begin by trying to define what jazz is and tell you that definition is very difficult. A lot of definitions *are* difficult. If you ask me what a pangolin is, I can try to describe it, but this may entail my using terms which themselves need explanation. It would be better to show you a picture of one; better still, to show you a real one going about its business. (By the way, it is any mammal of the order *Pholidota* found in tropical Africa, South Asia and Indonesia, having a body covered with overlapping horny scales and a long snout specialized for feeding on ants and termites; also called a **scaly anteater**.)

So, if you seek an understanding of jazz, you should certainly listen to it on recordings and on the radio, watch it on film, on TV and live and, if you have the means and opportunity, try playing it yourself. I'm here to help you to listen to, watch and play the 'right' things and to know why they are 'right'.

Music is sound, so listening is of supreme importance. All the pioneers of jazz had to listen – that was the way in which the music was copied and developed and handed on in the absence of written or recorded material.

To define jazz, I need to use terms which themselves need explaining, but I will give a definition now and return to the subject later. Jazz is a type of music which differs in at least three ways from non-jazz:

1   In jazz, the player is of far more importance than in non-jazz; jazz depends more on interpretation by individuals than on adherence to a score. I know that orchestral soloists and conductors 'interpret', but they do so within constraints. Sir Peter Hall suggested that, if classical music is the search for anonymous perfection, jazz is about individuality. André Previn is quoted as saying: 'The basic difference between classical music and jazz is that in the former the music is always greater than the performance – whereas the way jazz is performed is always more important than what is being played.'

2   Carrying the first point even further, jazz invites – depends on – not only *improvisation* but *collective improvisation* by several players at once.

3   Finally, because jazz is a freer music, the rhythms may become very complicated – and note that there is a difference between 'rhythm' (what the music is doing) and 'beat' (the steady pulse on which it does it).

Jazz and the six senses

Jazz is predominantly a matter of listening, but I want you to remember that there may be other clues which will (perhaps unexpectedly) give you information about what you are hearing. Sight plays a part in live music: watching the players and how they interact with one another and the audience. This can be especially important in establishing or reinforcing a piece; after 50 years, the inspired playing of a trombonist at a gig just after his parents had been killed in a car crash still haunts me. Touch is certainly important if you are a musician – and you should not overlook smell and even taste. As a pianist, I find the smells of pianos highly evocative of certain occasions and this may help to shape my enjoyment (or otherwise) of an event. Taste, I admit, seems a little remote in this context, but the anticipation of a Madras prawn and mushroom after a *gig* (performance), or the memory of the one you had last time, may well affect your attitude towards the *last set* (tunes between the last interval and the end of the gig).

The sixth – sometimes called the kinaesthetic – sense (that which enables us to perceive the relative and changing positions of parts of our body) is the one that enables the musician to play 'without thinking' – or, at least, without having to think what to do to produce a desired note or pattern of notes. In the early stages of playing any instrument in any style, it is well known that the need to instruct the muscles to do the right things at the right times overrides any possibility of playing smoothly. Once you can either read, or hear in your mind's ear, a note or pattern of notes and then play what you want without further ado, you have achieved a great leap forward.

As we shall see, jazz emerged from definable roots as a music which began to sound different from anything that had been heard before, but we mustn't lose sight of the fact – as adverse (as opposed to constructive) critics were liable to until comparatively recently – that jazz is a part of the world of music as a whole. Jazz spent a lot of its childhood being ignored, derided or denounced as decadent. For example, the supposedly objective Funk & Wagnall *Desk Standard Dictionary* (1920) defines 'jazzband' as: 'A company of musicians who play rag-time music in discordant tones on various instruments, as the banjo, saxophone, trombone, flageolet, drum and piano.'

At school, our music master refused to accept that jazz had any artistic merit; thinking back, I'm sure that he had no idea how it worked. We were allowed to form what was called a jazz club, which held record sessions from time to time, but we had to be on our very best behaviour lest we should do anything which might be interpreted as emanating from the decadence 'known' to be associated with the music. Thinking back some more, I realize that this attitude actually caused us to feel decadent when listening to the music, while having no idea why we should – after all, it was only jolly music.

This view of jazz in what was then the 'older generation' was widespread until a newer generation of music teachers (and enlightened heads), who recognized a whole range of musical styles as valid, took over. The widespread interaction between jazz and the rest of the musical world on the concert platform has now penetrated the walls of the music room – and the examination room – at all levels of education. The danger with the modern attitude to jazz is that the excitement of listening to records and then trying to do likewise becomes a thing of the past. When the music is to be played from the dots and the performer is not encouraged to put the dots into an historical context by listening, listening and more listening, the music becomes flat and sterile.

Non-jazz

What should we call 'non-jazz'? The term 'classical music' (despite Classic FM) has a particular meaning: 'the period of the concert symphony and the concerto between the Baroque (ending in about 1750) and the Early Romantic (beginning in about 1800)'. We cannot complain about people using the word 'jazz' loosely if we ourselves contrast it with 'classical' music. Some use the term 'serious music' to contrast with jazz, but that implies, first, that jazz isn't (in its way) serious and, second, that non-jazz knows not how to amuse. The Chinese, I understand, call non-jazz 'noble music', an unusual term which seems curiously helpful.

The pianist Ahmed Jamal calls jazz 'American classical music', and Willis Conover is quoted as saying: 'Jazz is a language. It is people living in sound. Jazz is people talking, laughing, crying, building, painting, mathematicizing, abstracting, extracting, giving to, taking from, making of. In other words, living.' Read on, and see what *you* think.

The three elements of music

In this chapter you will learn:

- ▶ *about rhythm as exemplified by work songs*
- ▶ *about melody*
- ▶ *about harmony*
- ▶ *how to fit these three elements together to make music.*

I am going to relate the 'three elements' of music – rhythm, melody and harmony – to the culture of those who were to devise jazz.

The music we are examining had its origins in the culture of black people collected from Africa and taken to America, where those who survived the journey were set to work as slaves, many in the cotton plantations of the South. Imagine it – to be uprooted from your culture and homeland, taken you know not where, and made to perform alien tasks for people about whom you know almost nothing and whose behaviour towards you might well leave something to be desired.

You could be separated from everyone you know and all that you have is your memory of your homeland and your culture and the essential part that rhythm, music and dance played in everyday life. And so, if you had the opportunity, you would beat out rhythms and sing and dance, taking refuge in the familiar and perhaps being able to forget, for a while at least, the indignities you have suffered – *Nobody Knows the Trouble I Seen*.

Rhythm – work songs

Rhythm, music and dance were not only recreational. The 'language of the drums' is a very practical means of spreading information rapidly from one settlement to another. Many cultures have adopted rhythmic devices to aid work, nautical heave-ho songs – sea shanties – being an obvious example. And so the Africans sang 'work songs', to relieve boredom (as some factory workers sing at the bench), to spread (often subversive) information and, most importantly in the present context, to give a rhythm to rhythmic tasks – such as felling trees, breaking stones, driving in railroad spikes and so on.

Here is a practical exercise: clap (quietly) a steady beat: 1–2–3–4, 1–2–3–4 . . . a bit faster than one a second. I will represent this on a grid where each box represents four beats:

1	2	3	4	1	2	3	4	1	2	3	4	1	2	3	4
1	2	3	4	1	2	3	4	1	2	3	4	1	2	3	4

Now keep up the rhythm, but chant these work-song words in time with it:

Be–	e–	e	my	wom-an	girl,	I'll	be–	e–	e	your	man				
1	2	3	4	1	2	3	4	1	2	3	4	1	2	3	4

(The 1–2–3 relates to the length of the word Be–e–e; it does not imply an unsteady beat.)

Now try altering the way the words fall on the beats:

Be		my		wom-an	girl,			I'll	be		your	man			
1	2	3	4	1	2	3	4	1	2	3	4	1	2	3	4

Experiment with the almost endless ways of distributing the words in the 4 x 4 beats allowed, perhaps putting in a short 'uh', to help change the emphasis, for example:

Be		my	uh	wom-an	girl,	I'll		uh	be–	e	your	man			
1	2	3	4	1	2	3	4	1	2	3	4	1	2	3	4

Uh	be–	e	my	uh	wom-an	girl,		uh	I'll	be	your	ma–	a–	a–	n
1	2	3	4	1	2	3	4	1	2	3	4	1	2	3	4

In context – a work song performed to coordinate a task – a 'leader' might chant: 'Be my woman, girl', and the rest of the gang would join in on: 'I'll be your man' – described as the 'call-and-response' technique. The axes, or the sledgehammers, strike on the first beat of each bar, which will always therefore be a 'strong' beat. The tempo – 'how fast the beat goes' – will be related to the physical comfort of swinging the axe or sledgehammer. Comfort in musical tempo often relates to the dimensions of the performers; the arms as pendulums, for example, have some rates of swing which are more comfortable than others.

Listen out for recordings of work songs; luckily, some reasonably authentic material was caught or recreated before it was too late.

These examples show the difference between 'beat' and 'rhythm'. The beat is the solid 1–2–3–4, while the rhythm is the way in which other elements of the piece (in this case, the words) relate to that beat.

When written down (or, indeed, thought about), music has to have some structure and the usual structure is the *bar* (the unit delineated in sheet music by vertical lines between groups of notes). In our examples we are talking about 'four-to-the-bar' (1–2–3–4) music, which is by far the most common; each box represents a bar. If you relate the 1–2–3–4 pattern to a march tune (and surely everyone knows *The Liberty Bell* by J P Sousa through *Monty Python*?), you will feel that the first beat of each bar is strong, the third beat less so and the second and fourth beats weak by comparison.

The process of shifting the rhythm from the naturally strong beats is called *syncopation*. My dictionary defines this as: 'The displacement of the usual rhythmical accent away from a strong beat on to a weak beat.' However, we must remember that there are many other places than the weak beats two and four on which an unexpectedly accented beat may fall.

If this seems complicated, read on and come back to it again later. There is an all-too-well-known story that when 'a lady' asked: 'Mr Waller [Thomas 'Fats' Waller], what *is* rhythm?' he replied: 'Lady, if you has to ask, you ain't got it.' This story has been recounted often – more, I suspect, to avoid having to define rhythm than to raise a laugh. Telling the story enhances the mystique of rhythm as being something you either got or you ain't, enabling those who think they got it to adopt a superior stance if they so wish.

Melody and harmony

The other two elements – I might say 'dimensions' – of music are melody and harmony.

The melody is 'the tune' superimposed on the beat – indeed, the way the words fall will dictate the rhythm. We judge a show by its melodies – that we 'came away whistling' (good), or that 'there weren't any proper tunes' (bad). There are many memorable jazz tunes – or *numbers*, as we call them in the trade, borrowing from the music hall (US 'vaudeville') or the hymn board in church – and some less memorable. Less memorable numbers are the ones that seem (to paraphrase Sir Thomas Beecham) to last longer than they actually do. Most tunes last for 8, 12, 16 or 32 four-beat bars which are then repeated (see Part two).

If all the different voices or instruments involved in a piece sang or played exactly the same melody (i.e. in *unison*), the result would seem to lack something and that something would be *harmony*. Harmony is produced by sounding a number of different notes simultaneously – given that the different notes are chosen to produce an effective sound (if you'll pardon the subjective assumption).

The different notes chosen for a given harmony make up a 'chord' and the chords of a harmonized tune are arranged so that, although many different notes may be sounding at once, the tune itself is not lost – in fact, it may well be enhanced, as the notes of the melody are thus put in an harmonic context. We will explore the matter of chords in Part two.

Conclusion

All music comprises elements of rhythm, melody and harmony. Different styles at different periods may emphasize one element at the expense of another. The current trend in popular music is to build on a strong rhythmic element, which is in keeping with the listeners' apparent need to move in time with it, perhaps accompanied by flashing lights to reinforce it.

More extreme forms of modern jazz seek, it seems to me, to do away with all three elements, resulting in what we traditionalists call in our kinder moments 'amorphous music'.

3

The raw materials of jazz

In this chapter you will learn:

▶ *about precursors to jazz*
▶ *about the influence these different musical styles had on jazz.*

Few things arise from nothing; original as jazz may have been when it was first played, its practitioners must have been influenced by the many types of music they had heard. I have already mentioned work songs, a particular influence on jazz. Let's have a look at some others.

Nineteenth-century ballads

Traditional ballads (which are essentially sung poems or poems set to music) were brought to America from a number of cultures and continued to develop there. Some were performed for listening; others adapted for dancing.

Many homes had pianos and playing the piano was a fit accomplishment for a young lady. A whole range of instruments (including player pianos) are to be found in American mail-order catalogues from the turn of the century and, if Western films are true to life, the most run-down homestead had, Ah do declayre, a piano with an obligatory nubile daughter or widow (whose other accomplishments included flounced dressmaking and feeding hens) to play it.

In the days when home entertainment had to be home made, musical evenings flourished and forms such as barber shop emerged.

Traditional/popular music

Apart from the ballads, there was – and is – a vast body of other traditional/popular music which we should consider as a separate raw material. European – and especially French, Irish, Scottish and Spanish – popular music made a particular contribution to jazz. At first, it was performed locally by the immigrants who brought it to America; some of the performers had been, or became, professional entertainers and the music spread over a wider area. Soon, there emerged a body of entertainment music, a fusion of cultures, culminating in the now politically incorrect 'minstrel shows' with their vaudeville (music hall) mixture of songs happy and sad, light and thoughtful and musical numbers – featuring banjo virtuosi, for example – and other turns such as the now even more politically incorrect comedians Messrs Rastus and Bones. Firmly dedicated to authenticity, the HPA (Heritage Protection Association) is an organization based in Georgia, USA, dedicated to retaining the traditional words of, for example, plantation songs: words such as 'darkie', 'massa', 'de oberseer' and so on.

The interplay between the demand for and the development of entertainment spread what already existed and provided an impetus for new material and a growing body of performers.

Religious music

America was an ideal land for the evangelical, nonconformist missionaries, and the type of music they favoured was perhaps more abandoned than that in the conventional hymnal, although it followed the same musical pattern. Again, this was a travelling music and its influence was widespread; it spoke particularly to the black slaves, many of whose masters encouraged an active interest in the Christian religion. It was an obvious opportunity for music and movement carrying, as it did, a tacit seal of approval.

Black participants developed church music into a new form – the gospel song. Gospel singing often uses, among other techniques, the call and response of the work song, but its development had little to do with the mainstream of jazz development. The form eventually became absorbed into jazz via more modern developments such as rhythm & blues and soul.

Brass bands

The music of the brass band is an essential part of army life, of which there was plenty in America – particularly at the time of the Civil War in the first half of the 1860s. Brass bands (both military and civil) had three effects: first, they inspired their listeners (everyone loves a marching band); second, they made instruments available; third, they offered opportunities for people to learn to play.

The once prevalent idea that retreating Civil War armies left literally heaps of musical instruments behind them, to be fallen on eagerly by musical black slaves in the course of being emancipated, seems somewhat suspect. However, surplus instruments did become available and brass band music continued to be written and played, inspiring the young John Philip Sousa (1854–1933) to his spectacular contributions to the art – the precision, the tunes, the sousaphone.

'Serious' music

We must not forget that, as in any community, there were in America composers writing music outwith the foregoing categories. They would, of course, fall under the same influences, but would see themselves as aspiring American Chopins, Liszts or (later) Elgars. Listen particularly to the American composer Louis Moreau Gottschalk (1829–69), whose music evokes 'the vitality, grace and *élan* of nineteenth-century America'. You will surely hear – admittedly with hindsight – elements of ragtime trying to get out, even at that early date.

Ragtime

As the nineteenth century drew to a close, the American musical climate – suffused with all the aforementioned developments – was pulsating with something trying to articulate itself and that something came to be called ragtime, hotly (!) followed by jazz.

Conventional wisdom here raises its eyebrows, for the conventionally wise have been taught that ragtime is a piano music and has 'nothing to do with jazz', but both ragtime and jazz emerged within a decade and the influences I have described in this chapter played their part in shaping both styles. However, there was one further ingredient – the blues.

The blues

'The blues is both a state of mind and a music which gives voice to it' (Paul Oliver).

The *state of mind* is the well-known 'feeling blue – depressed, miserable, low spirited' – a term which has been in use for at least 400 years. The *music which gives voice to it* is the blues.

The blues was an integral part of the culture of most of those who first played jazz; it and ragtime influenced jazz from the very beginning and made it what it was – and is. Remember also that the other ingredients didn't suddenly switch off at any point; they continued to coexist with whatever was developing and make their contribution to it.

4

The birth of jazz

In this chapter you will learn:

▶ *where it all began*
▶ *whether you really have to be black to play jazz*
▶ *why it is called jazz.*

The earliest form of jazz is generally believed to have come out of New Orleans at the turn of the twentieth century. Although many of the greatest (i.e. remembered) figures of early jazz were indeed natives of that city, or moved there at an early age, there is increasing support for the view that jazz did not suddenly appear there and nowhere else. However, New Orleans was an important centre and continues to be referred to as 'the cradle of jazz'.

If jazz started as a modified form of brass band music, New Orleans had no monopoly on brass bands. Neither is it reasonable to suppose that this particular invention, unlike any other in the arts or sciences, suddenly arose in one place. As we saw earlier, there was much interchange of ideas among performers, and a wide public must have had the opportunity to hear what was going on in the musical world.

All that can be said with certainty is that jazz (in the strict sense) is a generally exuberant music which seems to have arisen from a synthesis of the music of the touring minstrel bands and that of the marching bands, with the added influence of other elements of popular music. I see ragtime, emerging in the last decade of the nineteenth century, as an important element. As a form of piano music, often devised and played by trained musicians, it drew inspiration from the works of the European romantics and the music of the American marching bands, resulting in a syncopated music with a strict form suitable for feeding back to the marching bands.

Why 'jazz'?

Where did the word 'jazz' come from? It was originally spelt 'jass' which, we are told, was an alternative to the 'F word' for what couples do. According to the *OED*, the date of the word's first attachment to the music will never be known, but it is said to have first appeared in print in the *Chicago Herald* on 1 May 1916. It was then spelled 'jass', but within a year it had changed, via 'jasz', to 'jazz'. Ken Vail offers a 1913 citation from an article by Ernest J. Hopkins in the *San Francisco Bulletin* where he defines jazz as meaning: 'something like life, vigor, energy, effervescence of spirit, joy, pep, magnetism, verve, virility, ebulliency, courage, happiness.' Yessss! Jelly Roll Morton said he invented the word in 1902 to distinguish his style from ragtime, but then, he laid claim to many things, including the invention of jazz itself, and it does not explain how he chose that particular word. However, in the account of spasm bands we read of the emergence of the Razzy Dazzy Jazzy Band in New Orleans in about 1900. Surely Morton must have come across them?

It is quite easy to imagine a conventional marching band turning into a jazz marching band, playing marches in what we would now call a jazz style but was then called 'ragging it', which is where the term 'ragtime' came from. Black people have always had a wonderful fluidity of movement; there's plenty to be seen when television presents travel programmes and the like – or when you see it for yourself. A New Orleans marching band not subject to military discipline and encouraged by a Mardi Gras carnival atmosphere would make use of that freedom to move and play fluidly and – hey presto! – jazz would be born.

🔊 **'FRENCH QUARTER PARADE'**

Track 1

A studio version of the transformation can be heard on records of the *New Orleans Funeral* type where the band plays mournfully on the way to the notional cemetery and jazzily on the way back to the wake. When you listen to it, the jazz style of playing, leading to its own repertoire, seems inevitable.

Therefore, although conditions in the southern states of America at the turn of the twentieth century were favourable to the emergence of jazz, it would probably sooner or later have come into being somehow, somewhere. When you listen to a great deal of music of the pre-jazz age (and I'm lucky enough to be able to listen to a variety of music as I go about my business), every now and then you hear jazz-like snatches and cannot help wondering what sounds the great composers might have produced when they were experimenting and improvising. We shall never know, but the walking bass was not unknown to Alessandro Scarlatti, and Mozart, for example, might have hit on a species of ragtime which is lost to us.

After all, he was no stranger to experiment and wrote a set of interchangeable waltz bars that could be assembled in an order dictated by thrown dice.

The New Orleans myth, if we may go so far as to call it that, has arisen from several factors: a human 'need' to pinpoint origins, the accidents of birth of its musicians (a slight question begging there) and perhaps even an awareness of its potential as a tourist attraction.

Finally, we should not view early jazz as necessarily a purely black music. The influences which led to its flowering were many and varied and, given its origins and geographical spread, white people were involved in its early development and some played music in this new form. Neither, of course, are many people purely black or white. Jazz had considerable following in the Creole (mixed French/Spanish and black) population of Louisiana. Miss Lulu White, proprietress of one of the foremost 'sporting houses' of Storyville (the New Orleans red-light district), was 'noted as being the handsomest octoroon in America'.

There used to be a view born out of a sort of inverted political correctness that 'only black people could play jazz'. Doubtless there was a time when only those who had experienced the feelings that *lay behind* the music could express those feelings *through* the music, but later, those who had experienced the feelings at first hand had all passed on; the music would embody those feelings and would 'speak for itself', as you might say.

As time went on, new musical generations would come along who accepted the music as it was and couldn't be expected to have first-hand experience of what went into it. Whether black or white, they would be playing and developing what they heard.

Spontaneous generation

If you doubt that the same musical idea can emerge spontaneously in more than one place, I would cite an exuberant record that a group of friends and I made in the Cambridgeshire village of Swavesey in 1953. With hindsight, it is quite clear that we were playing what emerged from America two years later as rock'n'roll. If only we'd realized ...

Pioneers of jazz

In this chapter you will learn:

▶ *about the first recordings*
▶ *about the first players*
▶ *about early white jazz.*

For information on the pioneers of jazz we have, until the advent of recording, to rely on the memories of musicians. Who did what, where and when, and how well they did it, is often a matter of conjecture. It was generally many years after the events that the social historians of jazz came on the scene and the survivors of the early days to whom they talked tended to make extravagant claims on behalf of both themselves and others; these memories were then accepted or modified according to the preconceptions and biases of the interviewers and set down in print, thus giving them an often unwarranted seal of definitive accuracy.

Recordings

Phonograph records of jazz were not cut until a couple of decades or so after its emergence and only from that point do we have the means to judge it (or at least what got on to the records) for ourselves. However, from recordings and reminiscences we can form some opinion about which musicians made a significant contribution to the shaping of jazz and, in due course, we will look at some of the careers of those who came out of New Orleans and who were born before or around the turn of the twentieth century.

Their inclusion here is not to acknowledge them all as equally great and there would be a great deal of disagreement with any attempt to grade them. Their intertwining careers give rise to some repetition, but this helps to build a general picture of the bands through which the music took shape and to introduce others who contributed to the development. My final exhortation is that you should seek out recordings of all these artists and compare and contrast their styles and put them into the developing musical context.

The Spasm Band

It is one thing to acquire ready-made instruments; another to make them yourself. Home-made instruments include guitars, banjos and fiddles made from wooden boxes; comb and paper or its improved version, the kazoo; kettles and lengths of pipe played with a trumpet embouchure; large cans and jugs into which raspberries are blown to give fine bass notes; the tea-chest bass; and an assortment of bells, whistles and percussion instruments, including kitchen utensils, suitcases and the corrugated washboard played with thimbles or brush heads.

I am indebted to Owen Bryce who sent me this passage from *The French Quarter* (Herbert Osburg, 1936):

> One of the most popular of these combinations, though not for dancing, was a company of boys from 12 to 15 years old who called themselves the Spasm Band. They were the real creators of jazz and the Spasm Band was the original jazz band. There were seven members besides the manager and the principal organiser, Harry Gregson, who was the singer of the outfit: he crooned the popular songs of the day through a piece of gas-pipe since he couldn't afford a proper megaphone. The musicians were Emile Lacomb, otherwise known as Stalebread Charley, who played a fiddle made out of a cigar-box; Willie Bussey, better known as Cajun, who performed upon the harmonica; Charley Stein who manipulated an old kettle, a cowbell, a gourd filled with pebbles and other traps and in later life became a famous drummer; Chinee, who smote the bull fiddle, at first half a barrel and later a coffin-shaped contraption built by the boys; Warm Gravy; Emile Benrod, called Whiskey; and Frank Bussey, known as Monk 1. The last three played whistles and various horns, most of them home made, and each had at least three instruments upon which he alternated. The Spasm Band first appeared in New Orleans about 1895 [and toured with Doc Malney's Minstrel Show]. Their big moment came when they serenaded Sarah Bernhardt who expressed amazement and gave them each a coin. They were then billed as the Razzy Dazzy Spasm Band.

> About 1900 another band appeared with the same name and the original band made violent protest so the band repainted their placards to read Razzy Dazzy Jazzy Band! Thus it began… and now look!

The spasm bands were important in that they encouraged the making of music, however primitive; for example, it was with such a band that Edward 'Kid' Ory earned the money to buy his first trombone. In the 1920s, such masters as the clarinettist Johnny Dodds played with spasm bands, or skiffle groups as they came to be called, in Chicago, making an extremely enjoyable and exciting noise with a mixture of conventional and improvised instruments. The 1950s saw a new (and incomparable with the old) skiffle emerge which, although somewhat tiresome in its relentlessness, surely did more good than harm in encouraging aspiring young musicians to get started and perhaps to move on to better (?) things.

The first 'jass' band

According to musicians' memories, the first band to play jazz – before it was even given that name – in New Orleans was that led by Charles 'Buddy' Bolden (1877–1931), barber, scandal-sheet editor and cornettist who 'blew his brains out through his horn' and spent his life from 1907 in a mental hospital. Bolden appears to have been a band agent as well as a player; he would tour the venues of his bands and sit in with them, playing a fine, powerful cornet, doubtless strengthened in the minds of those who heard him – and certainly of those who did not – by nostalgia.

In the only known photograph of Bolden's band, taken before 1895, we see Bolden on cornet, Willie Warner and Frank Lewis on clarinets, Willie Cornish on valve trombone, violin and drums, Brock Mumford on guitar and Jimmy Johnson on string bass.

An even rarer piece of Boldeniana than the photograph is a wax cylinder recording of the band – so rare is it that its existence has never been proved, but it is a delightful legend kept alive by writers and lecturers on jazz (it's an unwritten law that you have to mention it!). In the absence of this vital evidence, what sort of music might Bolden have played? The presence of the guitar (possibly) and the double bass (certainly) implies that the group photographed was not a marching band and Bolden's reported use of a violin in addition suggests that his music was a fusion of minstrel and marching traditions. Bolden himself described his music as ragtime.

Joe 'King' Oliver

Joe Oliver (1885–1938) was born somewhere in Louisiana; he moved to New Orleans as a boy and studied first the trombone and then the cornet, which remained his instrument thereafter. He played in several New Orleans bands, and led his own, until he moved to Chicago in 1918. Before the move he played in Kid Ory's Band and it was Ory who named him 'King'.

In Chicago, he played with both Lawrence Duhé and Bill Johnson, eventually taking over the former's band which emerged as King Oliver's Creole Jazz Band and which held a legendary position in the world of jazz until 1924. Many of the best jazz musicians of the day played for or with Oliver at one time or another; the Creole Jazz Band included Louis Armstrong and Johnny Dodds.

In its time, King Oliver's Creole Jazz Band produced a sound of collective improvisation which has seldom been bettered and, being the first black band to record (1923), its sound is enshrined for ever. The very quintessence of New Orleans music is here – the two cornets (Oliver and Armstrong) playing the melody, with Oliver's unique use of mutes; the lower voice filled with Honoré Dutrey's trombone; Dodds's clarinet fluently filling the higher voice of the band. The emphasis was on the collective sound, as it is in a marching band; solos were not a feature of earlier jazz. The real excitement is to be found in the Oliver–Armstrong two-cornet breaks, different every time. The secret lay in the very close mental rapport between the two men: it is said that Oliver would quietly sing his next idea into Armstrong's ear so that they could have the harmony all worked out when the time came for the execution.

The Creole Jazz Band rhythm section comprised Bud Scott (an equal of Johnny St Cyr on banjo), Lil Hardin (piano) and Baby Dodds (drums).

After the Creole Jazz Band broke up, Oliver formed his Dixie Syncopators which flourished and recorded for two years. In 1928 he moved to New York, but it was the end of his years of genius: a brass player needs a good *embouchure* and Oliver suffered much from dental problems. He retired from music, settled in Savannah, Georgia and died in obscurity before reaching the age of 53, in 1938.

Freddie Keppard

King Oliver's was the first black band to record, but the honour could have fallen to Freddie Keppard (1890–1933) in 1916 had that trumpeter not feared that to record was to lay his music open to copying – a fear which seems akin to the belief that the camera steals part of the subject's soul. No doubt gramophone records have taught a great deal to aspiring musicians, from Charlie Parker downwards, but they have also created audiences eager to hear the real thing and provided enormous royalties for the luckier performers. Unfortunately, by the time Keppard did decide to record, he was past it; we shall never know what he sounded like in his prime.

Keppard was born in New Orleans in 1890 and his early career followed much the same pattern as King Oliver's: brass bands in his native city and a move to Chicago. He and Oliver were the two most influential New Orleans horn players during the emergence of jazz. He spent the 1920s in Chicago, playing with many of the well-known bands, including Charlie 'Doc' Cook's Dreamland Orchestra and Erskine Tate's Vendome Orchestra. He died in 1933 after some years of failing health.

Jelly Roll Morton

In a brief survey of those who were part of New Orleans jazz in its formation, whom should we leave out? Certainly not Ferdinand 'Jelly Roll' Morton (1890–1941), for he was one of the few who contributed uniquely to jazz. Most people recognize his genius – as well as the extravagance of his claims and imagination which antagonized many during his life.

Morton was born in Gulfport, Louisiana in 1890 (although earlier accounts say 1885) and had some musical training, first on the guitar and later on the piano. His father played the trombone and this is reflected in Jelly Roll's strong left-hand playing. At the beginning of the twentieth century he found his way to Storyville, the centre of New Orleans prostitution brought into being by Alderman Story in 1897. There was always a demand for 'professors' at the piano in Storyville sporting houses (as they were charmingly called) and Morton was one of the best. He started with the ragtime style (see Chapter 7) and developed it by bringing to it all that his voracious musical ear heard, his capacious musical memory stored and his nimble technique achieved.

Although Morton was able to play with a charming simplicity, he sometimes played rhythms so subtle that derogatory critics said that he had no sense of timing. He believed that the piano should, even when played as a solo instrument, be able to emulate a whole band and a comparison of his solo playing with the same compositions played by his Red Hot Peppers (1926–30) shows his belief being put, incredibly, into practice.

The latter half of the 1920s was Morton's heyday and he behaved larger than life – spending money whenever he had it and taking more interest in gambling than in music (Morton as the new Mozart?). His popularity declined in the 1930s but he was sought out in Washington, DC by Alan Lomax and persuaded (not, one imagines, a difficult task) to place the story of his life and his reminiscences on record for the Library of Congress Archive (1938). Taken with appropriate salt, these recordings give an interesting insight into the world of jazz seen through Morton's eyes. He moved to California in 1940, became ill and died the following year.

Morton produced a markedly individual piano sound and composed jazz of a type that has never been bettered. He played with many of the leading musicians of his time, although others couldn't take his claims that he had invented jazz. One of his contributions was to demonstrate the crucial role of the composer/arranger in jazz: he understood the music, he understood the instruments and he wrote for the musicians he chose to play with him.

Edward 'Kid' Ory

Kid Ory (1886–1973) was born in La Place, Louisiana on Christmas Day. He is chiefly – and rightly – remembered as a pioneer of the 'tailgate' trombone – a style said to have been named after the custom of placing the trombonist at the back of a bandwagon with his slide protruding over the lowered tailgate. This clearly enables the slide to be fully extended and encourages the trombonist to play *glissandi*. Ory was able to play many other instruments and, an early entrepreneur, he organized a five-piece spasm band which earned him enough money to buy his first trombone. His New Orleans bands featured at one time or another the brass of Louis Armstrong, Papa Mutt Carey and King Oliver and the reeds of Sidney Bechet, Johnny Dodds, George Lewis and Jimmie Noone.

Ory studied and worked in Los Angeles from 1919 to 1924 and then moved to Chicago, where he played with many of the top bands and made some of his most famous recordings with Armstrong's Hot 5 and Hot 7 and with Morton's Red Hot Peppers. In 1930 he returned to Los Angeles, played a little, then retired from music to help his brother on a chicken farm. At the beginning of the 1940s he returned to music, first with Barney Bigard, then with Bunk Johnson, and found himself part of the new interest in old jazz. Ill health forced him into retirement again in the mid-1950s; he continued to play and tour when he was able, but his playing was but a shadow of what it had been when he was in his prime. He died in Hawaii in 1973.

Johnny St Cyr

The banjoist Johnny St Cyr (1890–1966) was born in New Orleans. His father played flute and guitar and Johnny learned the guitar and banjo. His musical path crossed and recrossed those of his fellows in the Hot 5; he played in Kid Ory's Band in 1914–16, on the riverboats and with King Oliver in Chicago. He made his name with Armstrong's Hot 5 and Morton's Red Hot Peppers recordings in the 1920s, but he then became inactive and the start of the New Orleans revival seems to have passed him by. It was not until later that he returned to the jazz scene and the first and finest jazz banjo player was rediscovered. He died in 1966.

Johnny Dodds

Johnny Dodds (1892–1940) was born in New Orleans, taught himself to play the clarinet and in 1911 joined Kid Ory's Band with which he stayed until the end of the decade. He then went on tour, revisited New Orleans for a short period and then moved to Chicago, which he made his home for the rest of his life. In Chicago, he was a key member of King Oliver's Creole Jazz Band, being joined by his brother Baby Dodds on drums and, of course, Louis Armstrong. In the latter half of the 1920s, Johnny Dodds made a large number of recordings with many groups: classics of his style. The most important were those with the Hot 5 and with Jelly Roll Morton.

Dodds became less well known in the 1930s – during the Depression he joined his brothers in the cab business – but later he returned to music and made some recordings in the last two years of his life before suffering a series of strokes. He died in 1940 at the age of 47, just before the New Orleans Revival in which he would have undoubtedly been a key figure had he lived. To many, Dodds's tone and fluency is the quintessence of New Orleans clarinet playing.

Jimmie Noone

Of the New Orleans clarinettists who lived to record, Noone (1895–1944) was one of the greatest. He was born near New Orleans, moved there in his boyhood and learned to play guitar and clarinet. He studied the latter with Sidney Bechet, whom he replaced in Freddie Keppard's band in about 1910. He went on to play with many other great musicians – Papa Celestin, Kid Ory and Buddy Petit – and formed the Young Olympia Band with the last. Towards the end of the decade he moved to Chicago and played with Doc Cook's Dreamland Orchestra for much of the time, although he also played and recorded with King Oliver and the trumpeter Tommy Ladnier.

In 1926 he formed his own group at Chicago's Apex Club, notable also for the presence of pianist Earl Hines. He continued to lead bands, mainly in Chicago, and to record effectively from time to time. He never retired from jazz, although his popularity was eclipsed by the rise of swing – ironically, since it was he who had inspired Benny Goodman. However, he returned to popularity at the beginning of the 1940s, but died of a heart attack, a few days before his 49th birthday, in 1944.

Baby Dodds

Called 'Baby' Dodds to distinguish him from his older brother Johnny, this drummer (1898–1959) was doubtless the greatest to emerge from New Orleans, where he was born. He worked in that city, and on the riverboats with Fate Marable, until he joined his brother in King Oliver's Band in Chicago in 1921. He stayed with Oliver for three years and was then attached to a number of bands, notably Freddie Keppard's, until 1928 when he joined his brother and trumpeter Natty Dominique for two years at Kelly's Stable, Chicago.

He continued to play and record with many of his brother's groups until Johnny's death; he also helped another brother, Bill, in the cab business in the 1930s. Baby Dodds was part of the New Orleans revival of the 1940s, but a number of strokes curtailed his playing from 1949 and, although he continued to perform when he could, he had to give up completely in 1957. He died in 1959.

Louis Armstrong

Louis Armstrong (1901–71) was, to many people, the personification of jazz – and not without reason. He was born in New Orleans on 4 August 1901, although later legend had it that he had been born on Independence Day 1900 – which made him seem quintessentially twentieth-century American. He spent an impoverished childhood surrounded by the music of New Orleans and earned a little money himself by singing in the streets: how his childhood voice might have compared with the distinctive tones of his later years is worth a few moments' reflection!

On the eve of New Year 1913 he fired a jubilant pistol shot in the street, was arrested and sent to the waifs' home. It was here that he learned to play the cornet, inspired by his tutor in the home, Peter David.

After he was released, Louis played for various bands and during this time he met King Oliver who, of all of those who attempted to bask in the reflected glory of having taught Louis Armstrong to play jazz, actually did.

We tend to think of musicians only in terms of their music but comparatively few were able to make a living by their playing, so while Louis was making music in other people's leisure hours, he was also working hard during the day selling coal, milk, newspapers and similar goods.

Oliver moved to Chicago in 1918, saying that one day he hoped to be able to send for Louis. Louis stayed in New Orleans and took Oliver's place in Kid Ory's Band, working the riverboats and playing in street parades. In 1922 Oliver, who was playing at Lincoln Gardens, Chicago, invited Armstrong to join him as second cornet. It is sometimes suggested that Oliver was working on the principle that 'if you can't beat 'em, join 'em', but this reasoning must be somewhat unsound since Armstrong seems to have had no urge to leave New Orleans except at Oliver's summons.

After a couple of years with Oliver, during which time he made his first recordings (notable not least for their capturing of the fabulous two-cornet breaks), Armstrong left to tour with Fletcher Henderson, with whom he also played a six-month residency at the Roseland Ballroom, New York. In the autumn of 1925 he left Henderson and joined his second wife, Lil Hardin Armstrong, and her Dreamland Syncopators in Chicago. On 12 November he made the first of the Hot 5 recordings, one of the never-to-be-surpassed feats of jazz of that period.

During the next few years, Armstrong played with many of the top bands – Carroll Dickerson, Clarence Jones, Luis Russell, Erskine Tate. He also made countless records, for instance accompanying blues singers such as Bessie Smith. At the beginning of the 1930s he moved from jazz and blues towards popular ballads; he sang and clowned; he appeared on stage and film set; he became what would nowadays be called 'a personality'.

It is worthy of note that Armstrong, with his sympathetic pianist Earl Hines and drummer Zutty Singleton, attempted to run a nightclub in Chicago for a short period, but the venture was unsuccessful. Armstrong was no businessman, nor was he a natural leader – his name was made through entertainment, not from gathering talent.

He visited Europe for the first time in 1932 and again for an extended tour in 1933–35, continuing as a showman, one of the greatest ever ambassadors of jazz. He continued to tour the United States extensively until after the war, and in 1947 formed the first of the Louis Armstrong All Stars groups. He now started to travel all over the world, visiting London again in 1956; there must be few major countries in which he did not play. In the last few years his health was not always good, although this is hardly surprising in one who led such a strenuous life.

He made many film appearances, but his singing of 'Hello Dolly' in the film of that name (1956) is particularly noteworthy. Although he sang for less than one minute, thousands of people went to see the film just to savour that minute.

Louis continued to play until he suffered a heart attack in March 1971. He died two days after his 72nd birthday, mourned as one of the greatest jazz musicians of all time.

The Hot 5

There is no doubt that one of Louis Armstrong's most important musical achievements was assembling his Hot 5 in 1925–27, solely for the purpose of recording. The lasting popularity of these recordings has no doubt surpassed anyone's wildest dreams at the time.

Armstrong, on cornet in the earlier sessions and on trumpet in the later ones, was in his prime. In combination with clarinettist Johnny Dodds and trombonist Kid Ory, the front line whole was certainly greater than the sum of its considerable parts. King Oliver's band had specialized in collective improvisation; the Hot 5, with three virtuosi in its front line, concentrated on solos and offered a refinement of New Orleans jazz which it is difficult to better.

Part of the lightness lies in the small rhythm section – the banjo of Johnny St Cyr and the piano of Lil Hardin, by that time Armstrong's second wife. Although St Cyr was one of the finest banjo players to come out of New Orleans, Lil Hardin was by no means the world's best pianist – but at least she knew what was wanted.

In May 1927, the Hot 5 became the Hot 7 for one week with the addition of the tuba of Pete Briggs and the drums of Baby Dodds, Johnny's brother.

Early white jazz

It was a sore point for the many purists who asserted that 'only black people could play jazz' that the first band to record jazz was white: the Original Dixieland Jazz Band (ODJB). The truth is that in New Orleans there were white musicians as there were everywhere else, that they had their own marching bands, and that they played jazz. Granted, they could not have felt the racial oppression of slavery at first hand but, as time went on, that ingredient became diluted and the music found its own voice.

The general term 'Dixie' applied to the southern states of the USA dates at least from the mid-nineteenth century; it derived possibly from the word *dix* which appeared on the ten-dollar bills issued by a Francophile bank in New Orleans. The term 'Dixie Music' (or sometimes 'ragtime') was applied at the turn of the twentieth century to what we would now call New Orleans jazz. Because the word Dixieland became particularly attached to the ODJB, which happened to be white, its more general meaning was largely forgotten and it came to be applied, sometimes in a derogatory and dismissive way, to white jazz.

Anyone who does use the term 'Dixieland' for white jazz should pause to wonder why King Oliver named his 1925 band the Dixie Syncopators, why Coleman Hawkins described Jelly Roll Morton's music as 'Dixieland' and why Jay Jay Johnson applied the same description to Kid Ory's. Even if we allow a certain contorted logic to assert that both Hawkins and Johnson were (independently) being as rude as possible to Morton and Ory, it would hardly explain Oliver's deliberate use of the word to describe his own band.

The Original Dixieland Jazz Band (ODJB)

Papa Jack Laine (1873–1966) was born in New Orleans. He formed his first band at the age of 15, playing marches and the emerging ragtime music. He continued to lead and organize bands, notably the Reliance Brass Band in the 1900s whose cornettist, Nick La Rocca, became the cornerstone of the ODJB.

Bands have always thrived on interchanging personnel: the arrival of new musicians with new ideas helps to keep music fresh. This ever changing scene, while it makes the life of the historian more difficult, underlines the fact that individual musicians in jazz have far more importance, generally, than their counterparts in other fields of musical expression.

The ODJB was formed in 1916 after a disagreement among the members of Stein's Dixie Jass Band; the new leader was cornettist Nick La Rocca, with Larry Shields (clarinet), Eddie Edwards (trombone), Henry Ragas (piano) and Tony Sbarbaro, or 'Spargo' (drums). The following year this band made the first recordings of jazz.

The ODJB visited London in 1919; Emil Christian had replaced Eddie Edwards on trombone and Russell Robinson had replaced Henry Ragas on piano. The tour was not without difficulty: the band was booked to appear in the musical revue *Joy Bells* but lasted for only one performance as the star, George Robey, was upstaged (he thought – probably rightly) and got rid of them. The ODJB soon recovered from this setback and continued the tour, predictably giving rise to wildly mixed reactions from the critics. However, they played a command performance before King George V and appeared at the 1919 Victory Ball before returning to the USA the following year, leaving a legacy of the first jazz recordings to be made in Britain and an inspired younger generation with an even wider gap between it and its parents.

New Orleans Rhythm Kings (NORK)

The other acronymic pioneering white band was the New Orleans Rhythm Kings (or Friars' Society Orchestra as it was first called) which first appeared at the Friars' Inn, Chicago, in 1921 and disbanded in 1924.

The leader was trumpeter Paul Mares, born in New Orleans in 1900, who moved to Chicago via the riverboats. After this period with NORK he virtually retired from music, became a Chicago restaurateur and died in 1949.

The outstanding members of NORK were the clarinettist Leon Roppolo, and trombonist George Brunis. Brunis was born in New Orleans in 1902, played with Papa Laine and moved to Chicago in 1919. After his sojourn with NORK, he recorded sympathetically with Bix Beiderbecke; then (by way of a contrast) toured for over ten years with Ted Lewis. He spent the rest of his life leading or making an essential contribution to Dixieland groups until his death in 1974. Apart from being the first white tailgate trombonist and a stage clown who could operate the trombone slide with his foot, he did make a serious contribution to the art of sympathetic jazz trombone playing.

Leon Roppolo (or Rappolo) was born into a musical family in Lutheran, Louisiana in 1902. He was a highly gifted, self-taught clarinet player and ran away from home in his early teens to tour in vaudeville. The high spot of his career was his period with NORK; shortly afterwards, his mind failed and he spent most of the rest of his life in a mental hospital. He died in 1943.

NORK's drummer was Ben Pollack, born in Chicago in 1903. After NORK, he formed his own band which acted as a nursery for many of the leaders of the next decade, including Bud Freeman, Benny Goodman, Harry James, Glenn Miller, Muggsy Spanier and Jack Teagarden. From the 1940s Pollack became more of an entrepreneur than a performer, finally leaving music altogether to become, like Mares, a restaurateur. He committed suicide in 1971.

> ### 🔑 Ted Lewis
>
> Ted Lewis, clarinettist and bandleader, was born in Circleville, Ohio in 1892. He was first active as an entertainer rather than a jazz musician and the records of his 'orchestra' are not really considered to be jazz. His importance is that many jazzmen worked or recorded with him – including George Brunis, Benny Goodman, Muggsy Spanier, Frank Teschemacher and Fats Waller – so it couldn't have been too harrowing.

The Austin High School Gang

🔊 'BIX TRIX'

Track 2

From time to time a group of musicians comes together which contains a variety of emerging talent – which is not the same thing as a group of established, talented musicians deciding to join forces. (The Beatles spring to mind in the former context.) Such was the Austin High School Gang, formed in the early 1920s in Chicago, with such later luminaries as Bud Freeman, Dick and Jimmy McPartland, Frank Teschemacher and Dave Tough.

Born in Chicago in 1906, Bud Freeman was the first and certainly one of the finest tenor sax players of Dixieland, often compared and contrasted with Coleman Hawkins and Lester Young. During a long and distinguished career he played and recorded with many of the other undisputed greats of jazz. He died in 1991.

The McPartland brothers' father was a Chicago music teacher who taught not only Bud Freeman, but also his own sons, Dick and Jimmy. Dick was born in 1905, studied violin and later banjo and guitar, the latter with such effect that he was able to take over from Eddie Lang in the Mound City Blue Blowers. He was forced to retire from music because of ill health and died in 1957. Jimmy, born in 1907, also learned violin and later cornet; a disciple of Bix Beiderbecke he took over from him in the Wolverines. He continued to play, teach and tour extensively until his death in 1991.

Frank Teschemacher was born in Kansas City, Missouri in 1906 but moved to Chicago, where his clarinet playing was inspired by Johnny Dodds and Jimmie Noone. He was acknowledged as one of the greatest musicians of his school, but his career was cut short by an automobile accident in which he met his death in 1932.

Dave Tough was born in Oak Park, Illinois in 1908. He was a drummer of the first rank, inspired by Baby Dodds, but his career was continually interrupted by illness. His greatest periods were with the Chicago musicians at the end of the 1920s and during the swing era with Tommy Dorsey, Benny Goodman and Jack Teagarden. He died after a fall in 1948.

Bix Beiderbecke

Leon 'Bix' Beiderbecke (1903–31) was born in Davenport, Iowa. He started to learn the piano at the age of three and the cornet at 14. His introduction to jazz came from the riverboats which steamed as far as Davenport, and he was influenced by the riverboat trumpeter Emmett Hardy. At the age of 20 he joined the Wolverines and played first in New York, then Chicago, where he absorbed all he could from Armstrong and Oliver. In 1926 he met Frankie Trumbauer, the C-melody saxophonist, who worked with Jean Goldkette and Paul Whiteman. Trumbauer stayed with Whiteman until the mid-1930s, but Bix became more and more unreliable through alcoholism and left Whiteman in 1930. He died the following year.

Bix is probably one of the most discussed jazz musicians of his time; certainly he is held in a very high regard in which legend and performance are intertwined. There is no doubt that he made a significant contribution to jazz and that his inspiration lived on in Jimmy McPartland, Bobby Hackett, Red Nichols and Rex Stewart. It is also interesting to listen to his piano composition 'In a Mist' and to reflect that it was recorded in the same year as the first Hot 5 sessions.

The blues

In this chapter you will learn:

▶ *about the development of the blues as entertainment and as a strand of jazz*
▶ *about the development of rhythm and blues*
▶ *about the foundation of rock 'n' roll.*

The peculiarly African strand in the rope of jazz is the blues. We have already seen that the work song was a rhythmic chant to accompany labour, with a leader evoking responses from his colleagues. If we look at the form further, we find it was often used for passing messages among the workers or just for telling a story. The tradition of music as an integral part of life is clearly carried through here and owes little to any influence other than the African. It was from this type of music that the blues was developed, rather than from the combination of musical styles that produced ragtime and New Orleans jazz. The early blues is quite separate from that stream but, as it came into being, so was it taken into the New Orleans fold to enrich the material available for the development of jazz.

If we are at all familiar with the blues, we know that the words deal with basic inevitabilities – life and death, eating and sleeping, loving and losing – in the form of a poem, usually with 12-bar stanzas each of three 4-bar lines, of which the second is a modified form of the first, as in the examples. The metre appears free, but the singer fits the words to the musical pattern without effort; to some extent, this echoes the speech patterns of the blues singers. The rhyme is also based on the speech patterns; in Example C, we see 'line' rhyming with 'min[d]', and in Example D 'han[d]' rhymes with 'man'.

'Lookin' for my woman, well, she done gone off with another man' – 16 syllables to be fitted into nine beats. In print it looks banal – the blues has to be sung to take on its poetry and beauty and feeling and rhythm and rhyme, and no description on paper is a substitute for its performance, for it is (in its emergence, at any rate) a traditional music, handed down by singers who could neither read nor write words, let alone musical notation – which is, in any case, unable to cope adequately with the music.

Examples of different types of song

Example A *Work song*

Leader Did you hear about that water-boy gettin' drownded?

Response In Mobile Bay?

Example B *Gospel-type song*

L   It was one Sunday morning

R   Lawd, Lawd, Lawd

L   The preacher went a-huntin'

R   Lawd, Lawd, Lawd

L   He carried 'long his shotgun

R   Lawd, Lawd, Lawd etc.

Example C *8-bar blues*

I'm goin' to lay my head on some lonesome railroad line

And let that 2.19 train pacify my min'.

Example D *12-bar blues*

I walked all night long with my 32–20 in my han'

Yes, walked all night, 32–20 in my han'

Lookin' for my woman, well, she done gone off with another man.

The evolution of music is no different from the evolution of anything else; the original music does not die out because it has given birth to the next generation. The blues continued to exist and develop as a form, at the same time as it was making its contribution to New Orleans jazz.

The chief difference between the blues and New Orleans jazz is that the blues has a musical scale of its own – containing the so-called 'blue notes' which do not fit properly into our western scales, which are themselves fixed by the way our musical instruments are constructed. Of course, the instruments are constructed to play the notes of the appropriate scale, which is not, however, any of the blues scales. Fortunately, the human voice (and the slide trombone) can manage any note – including of course the blue ones; most other instruments can't, so a compromise is needed. The blue notes can be *approximated* by flattening the third and the seventh in the scale, but it is important to listen for the true notes.

This state of affairs would have been different had there been a fixed-note instrument with a blues scale, but nobody seems to have thought of making one – unlike, for example, the Scots, who have preserved their own pentatonic scale through the construction of the bagpipes. The need for a special blues instrument may have been obviated by the existence of the guitar, since it is possible to play in-between notes on it by manipulating the strings. The guitar was, and is, often used by blues singers to accompany themselves, and not solely because it is portable. Its ability to play blue notes is as important as the complement it offers to the human voice. The quality of blues accompaniment is to be judged by the interplay of the voice and instrumental answering phrase.

In Part two we will look at the blues structure (8-bar, 16-bar and 12-bar forms); in the following section we will concentrate on the 12-bar form only, as it is by far the most common.

12-bar blues

A (1–4)	I combed her hair, even manicured her finger nails
A (5–8)	Yes, I combed her hair, manicured her finger nails
B (9–12)	Ev'ry time I get in trouble, she let me go to jail.

The rationale behind the repeated A line of the 12-bar blues is said to be that, because it is a spontaneous music, repetition gives the singer–composer time to devise the B line while singing the repeat, but that may be an oversimplification.

In listening to blues – which is, as always, an essential activity since no amount of description will do the form justice – you will notice that the words of each line do not fill the whole four-bar musical accompaniment. Most of the last two bars of each four-bar section are filled by the accompanist's framing of some appropriate musical answer to the singer's phrasing, providing an effect which can be very beautiful. Although such integration took some time to reach perfection, it clearly makes for a very tidy, not to say delicate, form. It may therefore be the development of the form which decided the repeat of the line, rather than vice versa.

Types of blues

Nowadays, the title 'blues' may be applied to many different forms of music. So far, I have been referring particularly to the stream of blues not affected by the New Orleans jazz developments; what we might call the archaic blues. However, we do have to use our imagination when we try to find out what the archaic blues were like, since time and commercialism have had their effects. The mere act of recording, as I have remarked, introduces artificiality.

The other senses in which the word 'blues' may be used are the styles that I classify as rural, urban and general blues.

Rural blues is as much of the archaic blues as can remain when its performers have had the opportunity to obtain reasonable instruments, listen to one another, exchange ideas and enter recording studios.

Urban blues is a developed form, which might alternatively be termed 'vaudeville blues'. It does not necessarily adhere to the 12-bar form and has words and a style of performance markedly different from those of the rural blues.

Sometimes the word 'blues' is used indiscriminately for the title of any number played slowly, or even quickly; thus is the currency debased. It may be even further debased by those who use the term to describe certain kinds of popular music which may have no direct connection with blues or even jazz.

Blues singers

One of the essential instruments of the blues is the human voice. Generally, the male singers are instrumentalists and the females are not. This is not just an extension of the fact that there were comparatively few female instrumentalists; it has always been an added artistic attraction to have a girl singer with a band and there is a difference in quality between male and female voices – and between black and white voices; it all depends on the physical structures of the voice-production mechanism.

Male singers accompanied themselves, almost always on the guitar, and sang – at least in their earlier days – a more rural blues; female singers were artistes in their own right and turned the rural blues into vaudeville blues almost from the start.

🔊 **'SOUTH SIDE CHICAGO BLUES'**

Track 3

It was here that technology made itself felt once again, through the medium of the phonograph. As long as there is something to sell to the public, manufacturers will find new ways of exploiting it and in the early 1920s the idea of the race record was born – a polite way of saying records of black performers aimed particularly at the black market. This, it was argued, would sell not only records but, naturally enough, phonographs. One of these instruments could cost as little as ten dollars but, once bought, you needed constant supplies of needles, not to mention records.

Buying the latest record became as much of a need then as it is now. This was good both for the record companies and for the performers (exploitation apart), who found new audiences, especially in vaudeville, wanting to hear the real thing.

A blues boom was born with the release of Mamie Smith's record 'Crazy Blues' (1920), which sold over a million copies in its first six months, and the amount of recorded blues material from this decade is enormous. This is fortunate, for it allows us to hear not only the singers, but their accompanists, many of whom were as great, if not greater, in their own right.

Almost all the male singers of the more archaic blues were also instrumentalists, as I pointed out earlier, and the instrument they play is usually the one capable (in the right hands) of echoing and complementing the singer's voice – the guitar. (The harmonica is also capable of such impressions, but playing it precludes the performer's singing!) Possibly because they were able to provide their own accompaniments, male singers were freer of the influences which shifted the archaic blues from its roots. However, the more urbane the performers perforce became, the more their music was modified to the supposed needs of the public: it's a long way from Mahogany Hall to Carnegie Hall.

'Blind Lemon' Jefferson

Lemon Jefferson (1897–1929) was born blind near Wortham, Texas in the 1890s. He early began singing and playing guitar and built up a rich repertoire of some of the most primitive blues. In the mid-1910s he moved to Dallas, where he met and taught Leadbelly (see below); they played as a duo: Jefferson on Hawaiian guitar and Leadbelly on mandolin.

During the last five years of his chaotic life he recorded profusely and it was after his last recording session, in the winter of 1929, that he became lost in a snowstorm; the next day, he was found frozen to death.

'Leadbelly'

Huddie Ledbetter (1885–1949) was born in Moorinsport, Louisiana and brought up in Texas. He was a rough and violent man and served three prison sentences: for murder, attempted murder and assault. Not surprisingly, this roughness came through in his singing, especially in his recreation of prison work songs.

We have already mentioned his association with Blind Lemon Jefferson, much of whose work was as rough as his. Leadbelly played a 12-string guitar: his repertoire ranging from the authentically black to the worst pop ballads. He was one of the folk singers encouraged to perform and record by those indefatigable collectors of historic music, John and Alan Lomax, for whom he was chauffeur for a time.

In the 1940s Leadbelly played in clubs and went on tour, but was held in higher esteem by his audiences than by his fellow musicians. He died in 1949.

Gertrude 'Ma' Rainey

The spiritual mother of female blues singers was Gertrude 'Ma' Rainey (1886–1939). She first appeared in vaudeville in her native Columbus, Ohio at the age of 12; six years later she married William 'Pa' Rainey and the couple toured with the Rabbit Foot Minstrels. She first recorded in 1923 accompanied by Lovie Austin's Blues Serenaders and went on to make a comparatively large number of records with many accompanists (including particularly Louis Armstrong, Coleman Hawkins, Tommy Ladnier and Joe Smith).

Ma Rainey's recording career ended in 1930; she toured until 1933 when her mother died and she retired to Rome, Georgia. She died in 1939.

Lonnie Johnson

Lonnie Johnson (1889–1970), born in New Orleans in about 1889, was as much a jazz musician as a folk guitarist, but he did play and sing some very fine blues. He studied the violin and played the piano as well as the guitar. After an early visit to London he worked on the riverboats until the mid-1920s, when he started recording as the result of his wining first prize in a blues contest in St Louis. From the early 1930s until his death in 1970 his career moved in and out of music. Some of his best work is to be heard with Armstrong, Ellington, the guitarist Eddie Lang and as an accompanist to a number of blues singers, including himself.

William Lee Conley 'Big Bill' Broonzy

One of the most prolific and authentic (subject to the usual provisos) blues singers and guitarists was Big Bill Broonzy (1893–1958), who was born in Scott, Missouri. His musical career started on a home-made violin; it was not until the early 1920s, when he moved to Chicago, that he was taught to play the guitar by Papa Charlie Jackson.

By the mid-1920s Broonzy was making records and his powerful authenticity raised him to the ranks of the best-sellers. He recorded under a number of different names, probably to avoid the constraints of his contracts, but his unique style is always recognizable. By the early 1940s he was one of the lucky musicians able to make a living by his art alone. In the early 1950s he toured Europe, where he was received as a legendary folk hero. Apart from giving a number of concerts, he loved playing to small groups of enthusiasts and I remember him from one very long party in a Hampstead attic in 1955. After a slow decline, Broonzy died of cancer in 1958.

Bessie Smith

Ma Rainey's chief protégée was undoubtedly Bessie Smith (1894–1937), born in Chattanooga, Tennessee; she was another Rabbit Foot Minstrel in her teens. She developed a majestic vaudeville blues style, but was virtually unknown until 1923 when the New Orleans pianist/composer Clarence Williams was sent to find her as the answer to the immensely popular urban blues singer Mamie Smith (no relation) whose 1920 recording of 'Crazy Blues' had become a best-seller.

Bessie's greatest years, when she became known as 'The Empress of the Blues', covered a comparatively short period (1923–28) when she made a large number of recordings with a variety of accompanists, notably Louis Armstrong and James P Johnson. After that, although she tried to adapt her style to public demand, she slipped from general favour, continuing a stormy and erratic career until she died in an automobile accident in 1937.

Lizzie Miles

There are several other notable female singers, but most of them were not strictly blues singers and they appeared with larger bands. A prototype of such singers, who bridged the styles, so to speak, was Lizzie Miles (1895–1963), born in New Orleans. There she sang with early jazz bands; she toured the South, visited Europe and performed and recorded with Jelly Roll Morton, King Oliver and Fats Waller in the 1920s and 1930s. She continued to be popular as an entertainer until her retirement in the year she died, 1963.

Ida Cox

Continuing our parade in order of chronological seniority, we next encounter Ida Cox (1896–1967), born in Cedartown, Georgia. She ran away from home at the age of 14, also to join the Rabbit Foot Minstrels. Her career followed Ma Rainey's in the 1920s: she recorded first in 1923 (just before Ma), also with Lovie Austin, and continued a long recording career with a varied assortment of top musicians sympathetic to her style.

In 1927 she married the musician Jesse Crump and went on tour with her own show. She continued to perform and record (in spite of a stroke in 1945) until the early 1960s; her health then deteriorated and she died in 1967.

Bertha 'Chippie' Hill

Another Ma Rainey protégée was Bertha 'Chippie' Hill (1905–50), born in Charleston, South Carolina. She sang with King Oliver in Chicago and recorded with Louis Armstrong in the mid-1920s. She was more or less inactive between 1930 and 1946, but then was rediscovered and made further records and acclaimed appearances until her revitalized career was cut short by an automobile accident in 1950.

Josh White

Even non-purists would recognize that much of the work of Josh White (1908–69) is a long way from the roots of blues, but at the same time there is enough to ensure his inclusion here. White was born in Greenville, South Carolina; his father was a preacher and his musical career began in the music of the church. Later, he acted as guide to Blind Lemon Jefferson, who greatly influenced his music. He moved to New York, where he first recorded in the early 1930s; towards the end of the decade he became a nightclub performer of increasing popularity. This had its effect on his repertoire for, far more than other performers, he used his art to comment on racial matters. In the 1950s he toured Europe, where he was as popular as Broonzy, to whom he formed an interesting contrast. In 1966 he retired from music after a car accident; he died three years later.

Sonny Terry and Brownie McGhee

These two artistes have to be mentioned in the same breath, as they were associated as a duo from 1939. Terry (Saunders Teddell, 1911–86) was born in Durham, North Carolina and became blind in his teens; it was in hospital at this time that he learned to play the harmonica, developing a unique imitation of the human voice, interspersed with equally individual vocal effects – whoops and shouts.

McGhee (1915–96) was born in Knoxville, Tennessee and was taught to play guitar by his father. After he joined forces with Sonny Terry in 1939 the two toured the world and appeared in numerous films and shows. It says much for their artistic integrity that their performance remained peculiarly rural in spite of commercial pressures.

Muddy Waters

The guitarist/singer Muddy Waters (1915–83) was born McKinley Morganfield in Rolling Fork, Missouri He was discovered by collector Alan Lomax and made some Library of Congress recordings in the early 1940s; shortly after this he worked as a nightclub artiste in Chicago and started to make commercial recordings towards the end of that decade.

He toured highly successfully from the late 1950s and led bands which played tremendously exciting blues. Not the least of his achievements was his influence on the course of pop music, via the late Jimi Hendrix and the Rolling Stones – to whom he indirectly gave their name. Although Muddy Waters used an amplified guitar and the 'bottle-neck' style of playing, he resisted the debasement of his work by commercial pressures while remaining highly successful.

W C Handy

No chapter on the blues would be complete without a reference to the much-maligned William Christopher Handy (1873–1958). Handy was born in Florence, Alabama, had a musical training and started to tour with a minstrel band at the turn of the century. He was one of the first trained musicians to 'discover' the blues form and to write down examples, and to the performers this was his crime – he was stealing 'their' music.

Handy did for the blues what Cecil Sharp did for English folk song – with, one must admit, as much lack of sympathy and understanding on occasion. Among the many blues that he wrote down, composed, arranged or published, the best known are 'Careless (Loveless) Love' and 'St Louis Blues'. Handy turned to music publishing in New York in the early 1920s and continued to work, although blind for his last two decades, until his death in 1957.

R&B

In about 1950, the term 'race music' became unacceptable for discriminatory reasons and was renamed rhythm and blues – R&B for short.

R&B was a revitalized form that rose to even greater popularity as a result of at least three factors. First, there was the vogue for discovering forgotten musicians – or those thought to be lost even if they were not – which brought forward many guitar players and, later, copyists. Second, the style, which was based on the 12-bar blues sequence, owed something of its beat to the tail end of the boogie boom; boogie, which had been inspired by rural blues guitarists in the first place, paid them back with interest. Third, the development of electronics allowed performers to make their sounds, which had earlier been quiet and intimate, fill a large hall.

Piano ragtime and stride

In this chapter you will learn:

► *about Scott Joplin and other composers of rags*
► *how ragtime inspired stride piano*
► *about the growth of larger bands.*

I suggested earlier that ragtime might be thought of as a staging post on the way to the jazzy marching band – indeed, some early pieces of band music are called 'rags' because they are to be played raggedly and the word 'jazz' hadn't been coined. Some purists imagine the cart before the horse and object to the word 'ragtime' being applied to other than the syncopated piano style which emerged at the end of the nineteenth century.

Ragtime contains elements both of the march and of European music, developed by the 'coon songs' of the minstrels and that popular dance, the cakewalk (which takes its name from a dance competition in which the first prize is a cake).

The best-remembered exponent of piano ragtime is Scott Joplin (1868–1917), who wrote a large number of rags; the genre was repopularized in the 1970s by a Joplin number called 'The Entertainer' (1902) which featured in the Newman–Redford film *The Sting* (1973). Joplin's ragtime was further popularized by the American musicologist Joshua Rifkin, who toured extensively and played impeccably.

Almost all Joplin's ragtime pieces are in flat keys and have as many as four themes. His first piece to achieve prominence was 'Maple Leaf Rag' (1899), named for the Maple Leaf Club in Sedalia, Missouri Joplin's home town. He had presented an orchestra playing in the new style at the Chicago World Fair in 1893, but it was 'Maple Leaf' that popularized the word 'rag'. Much of the credit for the popularization of Joplin's music at the time must go to John Stark, Civil War veteran and (among other ventures) music publisher.

After the World Fair at Chicago, Joplin made his way to St Louis to play in Tom Turpin's Rosebud Saloon. Turpin himself (1873–1922) was no mean composer and his 'Harlem Rag' (1897) was the first by a black composer to be published. Turpin and Artie Matthews were responsible for the St Louis school of ragtime playing, which built a more jazzy and barroom style on Joplin's drawing-room thoughtfulness. It was not long before other pianists, brought up in the New Orleans tradition – notably Jelly Roll Morton – absorbed the ragtime idiom into their playing and composition.

Other pianists who developed the ragtime style were James P Johnson, his disciple Thomas 'Fats' Waller and Willie 'The Lion' Smith.

Joplin was adamant that ragtime is 'not to be played fast' and many of his pieces are so marked or carry other markings such as 'moderato' or 'slow march tempo'. *Every* piece of music (not just Joplin's rags) has its optimum tempo for its circumstances and, generally speaking, playing as fast as possible for the sake of demonstrating the player's technical ability – or otherwise – cannot be recommended.

Some of the earliest recordings feature ragtime pieces (and there are many piano rolls by the masters of the instrument mentioned earlier – and others) and some of these have been transcribed on to disk.

As we saw in Chapter 3, ragtime piano playing was one of the important strands which showed marching bands a route to converting to jazz. In this chapter we will look at some important ragtime players and those who developed the style.

Scott Joplin

The name of Scott Joplin became synonymous with ragtime, but there were many pioneers before him to lay the foundation of his success and many other composers and performers. Louis Chauvin (1880–1908), for example, although little is left from his short life other than the memories of those who heard him, must be reckoned with as a performer to whom Joplin owed a debt. Tom Turpin (1873–1922) too, who owned the Rosebud Saloon in St Louis and there provided some focus for the development of a St Louis ragtime school, was in the top rank of composers and performers and is credited with one of the first published rags: 'Harlem Rag' (1897).

Joplin was born into a musical family in Texarkana, Texas in 1868; he started to teach himself piano at an early age and his achievements so impressed a local music teacher that he is said to have given the young musician free lessons. Joplin clearly had some idea of where he was going, as he left home at the age of 14 to become a performer of the music that was beginning to shape itself into what would later be called 'ragtime' – performing with his own group at the Chicago World Fair in 1893.

He then moved to Sedalia, Missouri, where he met the entrepreneur John Stark, who became his music publisher and to whom he owed much of his success. In 1898 Stark published Joplin's 'Original Rags' and 'Maple Leaf Rag'; the latter became an instant success. These were followed by dozens of others, but Joplin's aspirations for 'his' music were more advanced. He went on to compose full-scale works such as the ragtime opera *A Guest of Honor* (performed in 1903, but never published) and *Treemonisha* (1911). Both were failures and the complete lack of recognition which the latter received did nothing to encourage the unhappy Joplin; his health took a turn for the worse and he composed little more before dying in 1917, at about the end of the ragtime craze.

Joplin's music has a distinct structure and voice; it became immensely popular in the 1970s when 'The Entertainer' (1902) was used as background music for *The Sting* (1973) and *Elite Syncopations* (1902) provided music for an oft-performed ballet. *Treemonisha* has been performed from time to time and very moving it is, too. The flurry is over and ragtime is now an accepted part of the musical scene.

The development of ragtime in its 'classical' form was left to a few masters. Its contribution to the development of jazz was the inspiration its syncopation gave to brass band and to those pianists who adapted it so that the piano could take its place in the jazz band. We have already seen how Jelly Roll Morton made his contribution to jazz by the extension and adaptation of the ragtime beginnings, and there were many others who developed the style in their own way.

I should say here that one composition that put the word 'ragtime' on the map wasn't a rag at all: 'Alexander's Ragtime Band' by Irving Berlin (1916). It epitomizes a particular style and outlook, but it did nothing for pure ragtime.

Piano jazz

I should say a few words about piano jazz and dispel the idea that somewhere gained currency that 'it's impossible to play jazz on the piano'. Certainly, if you define jazz in a particularly narrow way, so as to exclude the piano, the contention must be true, but no one would surely accept such a definition nowadays. Another factor sometimes held against the piano is that it arrived in the jazz band so late. Perhaps it is forgotten that it *did* arrive before the saxophone...

James P Johnson

'STRIDIN' IN HARLEM'

Track 4

James P Johnson (1894–1955) was born in New Brunswick, New Jersey and studied piano from an early age. The family moved to New York where he met Luckey Roberts, a ragtime pianist who owned a bar in Harlem. It was here that Johnson was inspired to develop ragtime into a style which became known as (Harlem) stride, in which the striding is performed by the left hand, turning the regularity of ragtime into something much more **39** percussive and free.

Johnson toured the United States in vaudeville and visited Europe as the musical director of a roadshow in the 1920s. At that time, his excellence as a pianist was often overlooked since he devoted much of his energy to musical composition and direction. However, his recordings – notably those with Bessie Smith – show his great capability and sympathy as soloist and accompanist. He continued to compose and play until 1940, when he had a stroke. This limited his ability to work, but he continued until a paralysing stroke in 1951 left him immobile and unable to speak; he died in 1955.

Johnson was the inspiration for many other pianists: those who took the stride piano and developed it in their own ways – Duke Ellington, for example – and one in particular who became as much a symbol of ebullient musicianship as of jazz, Fats Waller.

Willie 'The Lion' Smith

Smith (1897–1973) was born of a Jewish father and black mother in Goshen, New York. His mother was an organist and taught him the piano; he made his professional début in 1914. He served in France with the artillery during World War I, where his exceptional bravery earned him the title 'The Lion'. After the war he settled and played in New York; he was largely unknown elsewhere until 1935 when a series of recordings brought him to the enthusiastic attention of a wider public. With James P Johnson, Smith developed the stride style of piano playing which influenced many others, notably Fats Waller, Earl Hines and Duke Ellington.

Edward Kennedy 'Duke' Ellington

'A PURPLE MIST'

Track 5

Perhaps the most illustrious and indefatigable of all jazzmen, Duke Ellington (1899–1974), was born in Washington, DC. Although he learned the piano from the age of seven, he does not seem to have shown any early signs of his outstanding musical ability and was set on a career in sign writing until his late teens. However, he did organize bands as a spare-time activity and moved to New York in the early 1920s where he was inspired by the Harlem pianists James P Johnson, Willie 'The Lion' Smith and Fats Waller. It was Waller who persuaded Ellington back to New York (after his return to Washington) where, after various vicissitudes, he opened at the Kentucky Club and then moved to the Cotton Club in 1927, the start of his real fame.

By this time, he had such excellent sidemen as trumpeter Bubber Miley, trombonist Tricky Sam Nanton and baritone saxophonist Harry Carney. The band started to record and broadcast and became nationally known. Miley, master of the mutes, was with Ellington from 1925 until 1929. Nanton and Carney, however, who both joined in 1926, stayed until their deaths: Nanton in 1948 and Carney, who outlived Ellington and remained in the orchestra led by his son Mercer Ellington, in 1974 – a record. Many other musicians stayed with Ellington for long periods – for example, Barney Bigard, clarinettist 1928–42; Johnny Hodges, alto player 1928–51 and 1955 until his death in 1970; Cootie Williams, trumpeter, who succeeded Miley, 1929–40 and 1962–75, into the Mercer era. Notable also was Ivie Anderson, who sang with Ellington from 1931 to 1942, when ill health forced her to retire.

All this shows the tremendous rapport between Ellington and his musicians; if there is such a thing as job satisfaction in the jazz world, it must have been here. From 1930 the Ellington Orchestra began to enjoy an ever-widening popularity, with success after success flowing from the prolific pen of its leader. In 1939 Ellington was joined by the pianist, composer and arranger Billy Strayhorn, with whom he thenceforward worked so intimately and with such rapport that their styles became indistinguishable. While other leaders' popularity and output varied over the years, Ellington's never diminished; he wrote innumerable scores of the highest quality, toured the world and had endless honours heaped on him; he was truly a giant of jazz. He continued to work until, interrupted by ill health in his last few months, he died in 1974. The orchestra continued under his son, trumpeter Mercer Ellington (1919–96).

Thomas 'Fats' Waller

Waller (1904–43) was born in New York City. His father, a church minister, hoped that his son would follow in his footsteps; his mother played the piano and organ, which her son studied. By the age of 15, Waller had become a professional pianist in cabarets and theatres and started to record in the 1920s, not only on the piano but also on the organ – one of the few and certainly the first to make the latter an instrument of jazz.

The development of Waller's style from that of James P Johnson (who taught him informally) can be clearly heard: Waller's left hand was so powerful that he needed no rhythm section. He was able to hold his own as a popular entertainer without debasing the jazz he played – no mean feat considering that much of his best-known work is a conscious parody and self-parody of Tin Pan Alley songs. Also, although he was not a singer, he turned that very deficiency to good use in his guying entertainment.

He toured the United States and visited England in 1938, where he made a great impact on music-hall audiences, but he lived hard and drank hard and was found dead in a railway sleeping car at Kansas City while en route to New York City from Los Angeles in 1943.

Count Basie

Another prolific pianist, inspired by the Harlem school and Fats Waller in particular, Count Basie (1904–84) was born in Red Bank, New Jersey. He was taught piano by his mother and toured in vaudeville in a vacancy he took over from Fats Waller. In Kansas City he joined the Bennie Moten Band and after that leader's death in 1935 Basie started his own orchestra which bears some comparison with Ellington's in that he was able to command similar loyalty from many sidemen. That said, however, his all-round musical ability is less than Ellington's, his popularity has been more variable and he has made less certain forays into uncharted territory. This merely shows that comparisons are odious and is not to underrate Basie's contribution to jazz and the popularity he enjoyed before his death in 1984.

Earl 'Fatha' Hines

Earl Hines (1905–1983) was born in Duquesne, Pennsylvania, of a musical family; his mother, like Fats Waller's, was an organist. Hines studied the piano in the hope of becoming a concert pianist, but turned towards jazz and moved to Chicago where he met Louis Armstrong. Hines developed a unique style, inspired by Armstrong and known as the 'trumpet style': his right hand playing runs and tremolos in a style which was the spiritual father of that of many other jazz pianists, but his innovation was so advanced for its time that, although it hardly changed through several decades, it remained fresh and never seems outdated.

🔊 **'YOUNG SATCHMO'**

Track 6

In the 1930s Hines led big bands and, looking back, must have found satisfaction in having nurtured many outstanding musicians, including Dizzy Gillespie and Charlie Parker. Apart from a spell on tour with Louis Armstrong's All Stars, Hines continued to play both solo and as a leader with an undiminished vigour, which led some to claim him the greatest jazz pianist ever. He died in 1983.

New orleans jazz migrates

In this chapter you will learn:

► *about the spread of jazz*

► *about enjoyment of jazz in the home.*

New Orleans

One important factor promoting the development of jazz in New Orleans was that, in 1897, one Alderman Story decreed that prostitution would be legal if confined to a designated part of the city – an area that became known as Storyville. In 1910 there were nearly 200 'houses of pleasure' in Storyville, as well as innumerable 'honky-tonks, barrel houses and gambling joints', all of which provided an enormous demand for entertainment. In 1917, in an effort to clean up America, the US Navy Department closed Storyville and jazz started to spread in earnest.

The riverboats

Although jazz found a ready climate for development in the multicultural New Orleans, it may well (as I said before) have begun to emerge elsewhere at about the same time; the popular musical climate was right for it. The closure of Storyville may have given its musicians an impetus, but jazz was not static, for there were already routes for its dissemination – the vaudeville circuits, the railroad and the Mississippi riverboats – which were far more than just a means of transport.

The Mississippi is one of the world's largest rivers and the most important in North America. Since it is over 4,000 miles long, yet falls less than one-third of a mile in that length, it is slow flowing and comparatively wide. From the late nineteenth century, great paddle-steamers plied the river; for commerce, passenger transport – and pleasure. If you're going to move a few hundred tons of cargo, why not add a suitable superstructure and move a few hundred passengers as well, entertaining them as you go? Many of the showboats were fitted with a Calliope (pronounced with four syllables). In time, many boats carried a jazz band as well and some of the best musicians out of New Orleans spent a period in such bands, before leaving the boat at one of the upriver cities, particularly St Louis, Kansas City (on the Missouri) or Davenport, on the way to Chicago.

The Calliope

The Calliope was a small steam organ which produced a jolly (although not always perfectly tuned) sound. Jazz pianist Jess Stacey recalled earning an extra $5 a week for playing the Calliope – danger money, perhaps, since the instrument (with less than two octaves) had copper keys rendered blisteringly hot by the 150psi steam that powered the beast and demanded that its player wore protective clothing against fallout – often of red-hot particles – from the boat's twin funnels.

Neither was the enjoyment of the music of the bands confined to the passengers on the boats; on a pleasure trip it was customary to stop en route so that the landbound could enjoy the entertainment as well. Thus the riverboats spread both the word and the inspiration of jazz and acted partly as nurseries, partly as free transport, to the musicians who migrated northward from the second decade of the twentieth century onwards.

Captain Joseph Streckfus owned a number of Mississippi riverboats and was – perhaps unwittingly – responsible for the development of many musicians (not to mention their translation from New Orleans to points upriver) via his talent-spotting bandleaders. Foremost among these were the trumpeter Charlie Creath (1890–1951) and the pianist Fate Marable (1890–1947), both of whom spent most of their working lives on the riverboats.

Neither Creath's nor Marable's band seems to have recorded at any stage, so we can only infer their quality from their long tenures and their top line-ups.

Chicago

With the Mississippi route open, Chicago became the great centre for jazz for a number of reasons. It was – and is – a very much larger city than New Orleans, with a proportionately greater black population towards whom, in the 1910s, there was a somewhat less oppressive attitude than in areas further south. The closing of Storyville in 1917 may have hastened the exodus, but Chicago was becoming an attractive centre even before then. The city had places of entertainment of all types, with what would today be called talent scouts always on the lookout for new attractions – and what better attraction than one of the new jazz bands?

The jazz scene then was therefore much as it is today: promoters providing venues, musicians becoming bandleaders and inviting others to join them, a constant flow of musicians between one band and another and endless gigs, seasons as resident bands and – if you were lucky – recording sessions and tours.

The recording sessions are particularly important, because the recording industry centred on Chicago, although it was not until about 1920 that it came into its own as a mass producer of a new consumer product – the phonograph – and the records to go with it. When the phonograph caught on it spread like wildfire. The 1920 recording of 'Crazy Blues' by Mamie Smith sold over a million pressings in its first six months and from then on there was a constant stream of musicians – both known and unknown – seeking similar success.

Big fiddle

There were other ways of 'makin' big money playin' on these here records', as Clarence 'Pine-top' Smith says on 'Jump Steady Blues'. The ebullient pianist Will Ezell, for example, was wont to claim travelling expenses from Texas, but it was suspected that he lived just around the corner from the recording studios.

World War I

There were other reasons for the migration north in the second decade of the twentieth century. Remember that in the years 1914–18 there was a 'war to end all wars' being waged in Europe and that Thomas Woodrow Wilson, 28th President of the USA, declared war on Germany in April 1917 in order to 'make the world safe for democracy'.

The preparation for and participation in this activity created a large number of jobs in certain centres, thus playing a significant part in the migration, so, although we may get the impression that jazz was confined mainly to New Orleans (whence it sprang) and Chicago (where the recording studios were) and all points between, musicians were soon entertaining audiences across the country from Los Angeles in the west to New York City in the east.

Conclusion

We have seen that jazz emerged in and around New Orleans as the nineteenth century turned into the twentieth and flourished there because of the cosmopolitan population and the presence of an official red-light district (Storyville). The music, and those who played it, spread along the Mississippi and its tributaries on the riverboats. As the number of jazz musicians increased, more and more jazz bands were established in more and more centres.

Travelling shows and the railroads spread the music still further and, in due course, a growing record industry enabled people to listen to the music in their homes whenever they wished. Jazz was well established when public broadcasting began and it gradually penetrated that medium – often under the guise of 'dance music' to make it respectable. By the time of World War II jazz was well known to – if not necessarily understood by – most people and was well on the way to becoming part of everyday life.

9
Big bands

In this chapter you will learn:

▶ *about the formalization of jazz*
▶ *about the creation of the big band*
▶ *about improvisation.*

When is a band big? How long is a piece of string? When a band is small and all its musicians know the tunes – jazz standards – there is little difficulty in co-ordination. Its musicians work to the chord sequences and develop, by experience, a musical rapport which enables them to improvise on these sequences. Many of the early musicians were unable to read music (and even today some amateurs are musically illiterate – often making a virtue of it), but the idea of improvisation as something sacred or magical in itself is misleading, for the players are constrained by the tune and its chord sequence and you will not be surprised to hear some musicians play the same 'improvised' solo time after time for any given tune.

The first great composer/arranger of jazz was Jelly Roll Morton and it is to composition and arrangement that we must look for our next development. Composition is not merely writing the melodic line of a tune; it shows also how it is to be harmonized and the different instrumental colours mixed. The act of composition must have some line-up of instruments in mind; in other words, the tune must be arranged for a particular combination of sounds. Arrangement may be a part of composition, or a separate act, taking an existing piece and adapting it for a particular combination of instruments.

The emergence of the composer/arranger – for the two arts are closely bound – had two effects. The first was that musicians who could read music became the rule rather than the exception (although this was self-selection). The second was that bands increased in size; once the full possibilities of arrangement had struck home, arrangers needed a larger canvas on which to paint – and thus the big band was born. Instead of one trumpet, one trombone and so on, *sections* of two or three of each instrument were introduced. Within a section there might be a *featured soloist* – an outstanding musician for whose improvisational talent the arranger could allow. Otherwise, the ordinary *sideman* would be a good reader who could interpret the intentions of the arranger to give the band its individual sound. Some musicians would *double* on other instruments, giving the band an even greater flexibility.

Inevitably, some doom merchants saw the development of the big band as the death of jazz and, if jazz is collective improvisation, that must be true. Contrariwise, the big band was a natural development and provided an extended and more varied repertoire: a wider than ever base for improvisation. It has also been suggested that the advent of 'written jazz' was an imposition of western culture, or orthodoxy, on an art form that had sprung from a different stock, but the technique of written music was freely chosen by many jazz composers and arrangers and their satisfaction with the resulting performances (which they often directed as leaders of the bands) suggests that the development was welcomed rather than resented as a restriction of creative freedom. Certainly, few would deny Jelly Roll Morton, Fletcher Henderson, Duke Ellington and many others who worked in this way their contributions to the world of jazz.

Whatever the arguments, there is no denying that the 1920s saw the advent of the composer/arranger – often a multi-instrumentalist, often a pianist. A new era, a new sound in jazz, was born: that of the big band. This development could and did lead to some fusion, and confusion, between jazz and dance bands.

Fusion and confusion

To gain respectability in certain circles, a jazz band might call itself a 'dance band' – or perhaps an 'orchestra', an even more acceptable word. The reverse held good as well: to be daring, a dance orchestra might pretend to play jazz. It may have been such activities that provided first-class whetstones for the axes of the purists. If there are any purists of this type still about, let them remember the words of jazz pioneer Jelly Roll Morton: 'You'd please me if you'd just play those little black dots – just those little black dots that I put down there. If you play them, you'll please me. You don't have to make a lot of noise and ad-lib. All I want you to play is what's written. That's all I ask.'

It usually comes as a shock to the novice to find that the first of the great composer/arrangers for jazz was Jelly Roll Morton and that the Red Hot Peppers were not a splendidly free, improvising group but a tightly controlled, well-rehearsed band playing in the recording studio just what their leader demanded, but perhaps the fact that such a free-sounding result is obtainable in such strict circumstances should give us heart.

The 1920s, then, saw the birth of the big band, with sections of players rather than individuals, but players who were often known to be jazzmen – Louis Armstrong and Bix Beiderbecke in the Paul Whiteman Orchestra, for example – rather than ordinary musicians.

Paul Whiteman

Whiteman (1890–1967) was born in Denver, Colorado and during the 1920s rose to fame by his purveying of symphonic jazz – which included commissioning and performing George Gershwin's *Rhapody in Blue*. As if this were not enough for those who insist that Gershwin's piece has nothing to do with the blues, Whiteman and his orchestra went on to make a film, *King of Jazz* (1930), following which the royal title adhered to Whiteman, infuriating those who insisted that he had nothing to do with jazz either. It is true that the orchestra may have compared ill with its contemporaries, but it nurtured such jazzmen as Bix Beiderbecke and Frankie Trumbauer; the Dorseys; Eddie Lang and Joe Venuti; and Red Norvo. Whiteman continued as a musical entrepreneur until the 1950s and died in 1967.

Whatever may be said about Whiteman (and a great deal is), he introduced a wide public to what they thought was jazz and, even if it was not, it must have made that public more receptive to the real thing.

Mildred Bailey

One of the features of any big band was its singer and Mildred Bailey (1907–51) was one of the first girl singers; she sang with Paul Whiteman from 1929 to 1936. She was born in Tekoa, Washington and was introduced to the Whiteman Orchestra by her brother Al who, with Harry Barris and Bing Crosby, had sung with Whiteman as the Rhythm Boys. Inspired by Bessie Smith, Mildred Bailey was the first white jazz singer to gain acceptance; she in her turn influenced other singers such as Ella Fitzgerald and Peggy Lee. Mildred Bailey married Whiteman's xylophonist, Red Norvo, in 1933; they left Whiteman and worked together for some years, parting in 1945. She sang as a solo artiste with many other bands, but towards the end of the 1940s her health deteriorated and she died in 1951.

Fletcher Henderson

I have already mentioned the pianist and bandleader Fletcher Henderson (1898–1952) as an employer of talented jazzmen. In fact, he was one of the first to demonstrate the two modes of the leader – first as a talent-spotter, then as one who could make use of that talent by producing arrangements suited to it. This quality must be borne in mind when we consider what makes a great leader, and it applies to all those we encounter in our journey through the world of jazz.

Henderson was born in Cuthbert, Georgia in 1898, graduated in chemistry and mathematics and moved to New York in 1920 to pursue postgraduate studies. However, like many scientists he was musically inclined and, instead of pursuing his studies, he started work as a song demonstrator; he then formed a band to accompany Ethel Waters on tour. By the mid-1920s Henderson had the first big band to make a name in jazz, which he led for a decade. A continual stream of luminaries passed through it, the most famous of whom was Louis Armstrong in 1924–25. During this time he also made countless records as accompanist to blues singers, including notably Ma Rainey and the non-related Bessie, Mamie and Trixie Smith. By the mid-1930s Henderson's orchestra had fallen from favour, overtaken by those to whom he had shown the way. He joined Benny Goodman, for whom he had written arrangements, as pianist in 1939, but this was not where his talent lay and he left to form his own band again – although this venture was not very successful. The 1940s saw him dividing his time between band leading, arranging and accompanying; in 1948–49 he toured with Ethel Waters – his career had come full circle. The following year he had a stroke and spent the last two years of his life inactive, dying as 1952 drew to a close.

Don Redman

Henderson came to arranging in the mid-1930s, some time after his musical career had begun. His early arrangements for the big band had been made by reedsman Don Redman (1900–64), born in Piedmont, West Virginia. Redman was a multi-instrumentalist, a child prodigy who joined Henderson in 1924 and became the first notable big-band arranger. It was he who introduced the big band 'sounds' that we now take for granted – such as sustained saxophone harmonies – and who combined lines written for particular musicians with the opportunity for improvisation. Redman left Henderson for McKinney's Cotton Pickers in 1927; in 1931 he took over the band of Horace Henderson (Fletcher's brother) and ran it until 1940. After that he spent most of his time arranging and directing until his death in 1964.

Chick Webb

The first drummer ever to lead a big band, Chick Webb (1902–39) was born in Baltimore, Maryland. He taught himself to play drums, worked the riverboats and moved to New York in 1925. He formed his first band there the following year and soon worked it up to a big band line-up. By the early 1930s he had built a tremendous reputation, especially among his fellow musicians, based on his unsurpassed drumming. In 1934 he discovered Ella Fitzgerald; from then on his popularity grew, but in 1938 he succumbed to tuberculosis and died the following year.

Ella Fitzgerald

It was Ella Fitzgerald (1918–96) who carried on the Chick Webb band after its leader's death until 1942. She was born in Newport News, Virginia, brought up in a New York orphanage and discovered by Webb at a talent contest in 1934. He immediately recognized her worth, bought her a suitable wardrobe and set her on the road to fame. After leaving the Webb Orchestra she became a solo artiste and from the mid-1940s she worked with the impressario Norman Grantz, who became her manager. She often sang with Basie, Ellington and Oscar Peterson, yet there was much controversy as to whether or not she was a jazz singer, since she spent much time singing non-jazz material on the nightclub circuits.

Billie Holiday

If there is argument about Ella Fitzgerald's classification, there is none about that of the legendary Lady Day (1915–59), born in Baltimore. Maryland. Her father played guitar and banjo with Fletcher Henderson in the 1930s, during which years Billie was appearing in Harlem clubs. In 1933 she was discovered by John Hammond and made her first records with Benny Goodman, but Hammond was unable to persuade Goodman to take her on as a singer. However, within a couple of years she had laid the foundation of her international standing as a recording artiste with pianist Teddy Wilson and, later, with tenor player Lester Young, with whom she had a breath-taking musical rapport; she also made scores of other recordings and appearances with orchestras such as Duke Ellington's and Fletcher Henderson's. Billie Holiday's private life (which, in an artiste, seems to be a part of public life unless you're very careful) was increasingly fraught with battles against men, alcohol and drugs. As time went on, the quality of her voice became more variable. She had served a prison sentence in 1948 for a narcotics offence and was charged with another (can you believe it?) as she was dying in a New York hospital in 1959.

Jimmie Lunceford

In its heyday, Lunceford's orchestra was noted as the best coloured big band of its time, and had the leader lived he might well have competed with Basie. Jimmie Lunceford (1902–47) was born in Fulton, Missouri and studied music with Paul Whiteman's father; he was a multi-instrumentalist, although when he became a bandleader he played very little. His first band was formed in 1927 and rose to tremendous popularity in the mid-1930s. Much of its success stemmed from its chief arranger, trumpeter Sy Oliver, who created for it a style quite different from those of his contemporaries. Oliver, however, left Lunceford in 1939 and this, together with more changes in the line-up (there may be some connection), led to a decline in popularity of the Lunceford orchestra. It continued, however, until the death of its leader in 1947.

Boogie-woogie

In this chapter you will learn:

▶ *about unadulterated boogie-woogie*
▶ *about the major players.*

Although it emerged primarily as a piano style, the origins of boogie may lie in blues guitar playing. It was, some say, the result of a pianistic attempt to emulate guitar playing on broken-down bar-room pianos so that the pianist could be heard above the din. It's easy to be dismissive of the style if you don't understand it, and there's sometimes a lot to dismiss even if you do understand it.

Boogie is an eight-to-the-bar style, often in the key of G, following the simple 12-bar blues sequence. The left hand plays one of a small number of repetitive bass figures, pounding a steady rhythm while the right hand develops sparkling ideas, usually one per 12-bar chorus.

That's the theory of it and, in the hands of the comparatively few masters, it's tremendously exciting. Unfortunately, its simplicity is deceptive; it's a limited framework and it lends itself to debasement by being played faster and faster and to band arrangements which pound loud, sometimes discordant, riffs to excite the punters. It may be no coincidence that boogie and swing rose together, the latter helping to deflower the former. Even some of boogie's best exponents fell victim to this approach, but if you've been whisked away from washing cars one day to a recording contract and a concert at the Carnegie Hall the next, I can forgive your protecting your new-found security by debasing your art.

Boogie remains captured in its proper – although often earthy – innocence by a few performers who were able to play it without debasing it.

Boogie-woogie

Where boogie and its name came from is uncertain. Wilbur Sweatman and his Band recorded '**Boogie Rag**' in 1917. The pianist Charles 'Cow Cow' Davenport (1894–1955) may have attached the term to the eight-to-the-bar music. The boogie-woogie may have been a sort of dance; there is little doubt that it first became widely known through '**Pinetop's Boogie-Woogie**' recorded by Pine-top Smith the year before his untimely death.

The *Oxford Dictionary* gives one meaning of boogie as a 'derogatory term for a black person'; this may have some connection with 'the bogey man' who has also been adduced as an etymology. In modern parlance, the word is used in such contexts as 'boogie on down' and 'boogie the night away' – clearly a dance feeling.

Jimmy Yancey

For delicate boogie, rich in its blues influence, turn to Jimmy Yancey (1894–1951), born in Chicago son of a vaudeville guitarist and a singer. Yancey was a child prodigy, a tap dancer who by the age of ten had toured the United States from coast to coast and by 20 had completed a two-year tour of Europe and retired from the stage.

He started to teach himself to play the piano at the age of 15 and entertained regularly until, seeking greater security than the musical life offered, he retired to become a groundsman at Comiskey Park, home of the Chicago White Sox. He was held in high esteem by his fellow pianists and was persuaded out of his musical retirement to take part in the boogie boom in the late 1930s, making several records of rare delicacy and appearing at a Carnegie Hall concert in 1948. He died in 1951.

Yancey made many memorable and moving recordings with his wife, singer Estella 'Mama' Yancey, although in some his accompaniment is more competitive than complementary. Some have called Jimmy Yancey 'the father of boogie-woogie' and although this is not really a valid title, he had not a little influence on the Chicago boogie pianists, and he has a secure place in the development of the style.

'BOOGIE-WOOGIE COCKTAIL'

Track 7

Not the least of his contributions was bringing together black and white musicians on the same platform, through his early trio and quartet, the latter with agile vibesman Lionel Hampton, pianist Teddy Wilson and drummer Gene Krupa. Thenceforth, musicians could be recruited on merit, rather than on colour.

Track 8

'SWING WITH BENNY'

Goodman and his groups played some exciting – swinging – music. Today, our longer historical perspective suggests that swing was a form of jazz played by dance bands of the 1930s; jazz and swing lived symbiotically.

Glenn Miller

Another biographical film, *The Glenn Miller Story*, was made in 1953. This, however, was less accurate than Benny Goodman's, since its hero had disappeared in 1944. Glenn Miller was born in Clarinda, Iowa in 1904 and played trombone with Ben Pollack and others in the late 1920s onwards, until forming his own band in 1937. By the beginning of the war he was immensely popular for his unique 'sound' and presentation – the latter inspired by Jimmie Lunceford's Orchestra. He joined the army in 1942 and formed an orchestra to entertain the troops; in 1944 he was touring and broadcasting in Britain and at the end of that year was sent to France to entertain there. He took off in a light aircraft, but it was lost without trace. Tragic as this was, his sound was not lost; the orchestra lived on under other leaders and its sound is also to be heard from reverent copyists.

The Dorsey brothers

Jimmy Dorsey, reedsman, was born in Shenandoah, Pennsylvania in 1904; his trombone-playing brother Tommy was born the following year. Their father was a music teacher who ran a brass band in which his sons played. Both went on to play with many well-known bands – including the Paul Whiteman Orchestra – from the mid-1920s until 1933, when they formed their own band. This was short lived; the brothers disagreed violently and went their separate ways in 1935, each forming his own orchestra, each rising to fame in the swing era. In 1953 they came together again when Jimmy joined Tommy's orchestra, but the reconciliation was brief because Tommy died in 1956. Jimmy took over the leadership, but he himself died the following year. The trombone player Warren Covington carried on the Dorseys' name until 1961.

Artie Shaw

Since Benny Goodman had already taken the title 'King of Swing', his rival Artie Shaw became 'King of the Clarinet'. Shaw was born in New York City and learned saxes and clarinet, played with various groups, then retired from music for a year in 1934. The following year he created a stir by playing at a swing concert with a string quartet – this must have been more of a novelty than a lasting attraction, for he formed a big band with strings, but it failed. He therefore assembled a conventional big band, which was an immediate success and, since both leaders played clarinet, he inevitably became compared and contrasted with Benny Goodman. The pressures of his undoubted success led him to disband for a second time, but he re-formed bands of various sizes and compositions from time to time: one of the most successful names under which he played was Artie Shaw and his Gramercy 5. The same commercial pressures forced him to retire finally in 1955 – to Spain – a victim of his own personality and popularity.

Lionel Hampton

The first jazz vibesman, Lionel Hampton (1908–2002), born in Louisville, Kentucky, started as a drummer. Although he led his own band at first, it was his membership of Benny Goodman's quartet that made him widely known and enabled him to re-emerge as a successful leader of his own big band in 1940. Although jazz purists would question the taste of some of his showmanship (*à la* vibes), nobody could fault his enthusiasm and his ability to inspire those who played with him.

Woody Herman

Reedsman Woody Herman (1913–87) was born in Milwaukee, Wisconsin and was a child prodigy, appearing in vaudeville as the Boy Wonder of the Clarinet at the age of nine; he also took up the alto sax at that age. After playing with various groups, he formed his first (successful) band in 1936. 'The Band that Plays the Blues' was the billing – everyone needs a shoutline – although its scope was much wider than that. Three years later came the million-selling record 'Woodchopper's Ball', still highly popular. In 1943 Herman reorganized, dropped the specific 'blues' title and emerged with his First Herd. Since then, there have been countless Herds and countless front-rank musicians have passed through them.

Charlie Barnet

Charlie Barnet (1913–91) was born in New York City. His parents were rich and wanted their son to become a corporation lawyer; he wanted to be a jazz reedsman and won. By the age of 16 he was leading his own band, which played on transatlantic liners; from then until the mid-1960s he led a series of groups, but played little after that. His band of 1939–45 was one of the most popular of the swing era, but he seems to be less well known nowadays than he deserves to be.

Harry James

Born into a circus family in Albany, Georgia, Harry James (1916–83) learned to play the trumpet with his father and joined Ben Pollack before he was 20. Late in 1936 he joined Benny Goodman and in 1939 left to form his own group. It was then that he started to play sweet rather than hot, which led many people to forget his jazz foundation. He retired from music at the beginning of the 1950s, but later returned to the scene, re-formed a band and toured Europe, playing in the jazz idiom once again. He thus regained his stature as a jazz musician and continued to play and tour, with great popularity among a new public; he died in 1983.

More boogie-woogie

We saw in Chapter 10 that boogie reached its height of popularity in the late 1930s, coincident with the swing era. One musical characteristic common to both boogie and swing is the *riff*, a musical figure repeated over and over again. The boogie riff at its best varies from one chorus to the next, building up to a climax at the end of the piece or dying away delicately and peacefully. By symbiosis, soon degenerating into parasitism, some swing bands borrowed the boogie form and, as suggested earlier, thus led it to the slaughter.

Others used the device more gracefully, for example, the Bob Crosby Band which enjoyed Bob Zurke's boogie expertise from 1936 to 1939. Born in Detroit in 1910, Zurke formed his own (unsuccessful) big band after leaving Crosby, and died in 1944 after having spent his last few years as a nightclub pianist.

What happened to swing?

In this and the previous chapter we have seen the rise of the big band and the emergence of the swing era, a musical event which can be dated very precisely. Many of the most popular musicians of the swing era continued to play for many years and audiences became accustomed to sounds which were once new and exciting. This is not to say that later musicians lacked zest and excitement – just that, as ever, our ears became accustomed to their offerings.

to band (particularly notable: Billy Eckstine and Earl Hines) until bop emerged in the 1940s and, with it, the name of Dizzy Gillespie. He then formed bands of his own and took the new music on tour, but was always forced to include some more familiar – and thus more understandable – music in his programmes. Nowadays, much early bop is itself so familiar as to pass unnoticed.

As Armstrong had said something new in the 1920s, so did Gillespie in the 1940s. Perhaps the high spot of his recognition came in 1956 when the US government sent him on the first subsidized goodwill tour as an ambassador of jazz, just one of many honours he received in recognition of his contribution to music. One of the articulate modern school, he shared and developed his music with students at seminars, a far cry from those musicians whose attitude often seems to have been to prevent copyists at all costs.

Charlie Parker

Charlie Parker's (1920–55) career was tragically short. He was born in Kansas City, Kansas and brought up in the other Kansas City, Missouri. His mother bought him an alto saxophone when he was 11; four years later he had left school and started his musical career somewhat disastrously, sitting in with a local band, playing very badly and being forcibly ejected. Far from being permanently discouraged, he vowed that he would go away, learn all he could and return to redeem his reputation. Few people could have done such a thing as magnificently as Parker did; he not only mastered his instrument, he became a first-rate composer and arranger and played an essential part in the forging of bop. He met Dizzy Gillespie in the early 1940s; both men had been thinking musically along the same lines – as had countless others less well known – but by 1946 Parker, who had been a drug addict since leaving school, was in bad health, exacerbated by adverse criticism of his music. He went into Camarillo State Hospital to be cured; after six months he was released and continued to tour and play until the early 1950s when his health deteriorated again; he died in 1955.

Kenny Clarke

I mentioned the interchange of the roles of the bass drum and the cymbal in bop. Kenny Clarke (1914–85), born into a musical family in Pittsburgh, was one of the pioneers of this style. He was a multi-instrumentalist who played with Roy Eldridge – the Gillespie connection – and the Teddy Hill Band (after Gillespie had left). He and Gillespie later joined forces, which was not surprising, considering their common influences. Clarke later became one of the founder members of the Modern Jazz Quartet, with whom he stayed for three years before emigrating to France.

Oscar Pettiford

The original bop bassist was Oscar Pettiford (1922–60), born in Oknulgee, Oklahoma into a large musical family. He started to learn the piano at the age of 11 and the bass at 14. He toured with the family band (parents and 11 Pettiford children) until 1941. Two years later, he was co-leader with Dizzy Gillespie of an early bop group. Subsequently, apart from leading his own band, he spent periods with Duke Ellington and Woody Herman until settling in Europe in the late 1950s, but his health suddenly deteriorated and he died in Copenhagen in 1960.

Bud Powell

The pianist of bop was Earl 'Bud' Powell (1924–66), born in New York City, also into a musical family. He brought an extraordinary energy to the keyboard that was admired not only by his young, emulating followers, but also by his seniors. Such dynamism takes its toll; from the mid-1940s his mental health was uncertain. He worked in France during 1959–64, where he deteriorated physically as well, and when he returned to the United States he did little more work and died in 1966.

Thelonious Monk

Another pianist, extraordinary in a different way from Bud Powell, was Thelonious Monk (1920–82). He was born in Rocky Mount, North Carolina; his family moved to New York City and in time Monk found himself in the group that was shaping bop. Yet until the late 1950s he remained in comparative obscurity, perhaps because he is a musicians' musician, highly regarded by (some of) his fellows and misunderstood by most other people. Gradually, this enigmatic and eccentric man gained a following and in 1971–72 he toured with Dizzy Gillespie and others, playing as The Giants of Jazz. Later, his appearances were curtailed, both by inclination and by ill health; he died in 1982 but his work continues to inspire rising generations of young pianists.

Buddy DeFranco

Born in Camden, New Jersey in 1923, DeFranco was the only bop clarinettist of note, leading his own big band in 1951 and, later, a quartet. During 1966–74 he became leader of the Glenn Miller Orchestra with which he toured the world; since then he has turned his energies towards writing and arranging.

Jay Jay Johnson

The bop trombonist was Jay Jay Johnson (1924–2001), born in Indianapolis, Indiana. He started studying the piano but changed to the trombone at the age of 14 and acquired a facility on the slide which until then had been attainable only by valves. In spite of his formidable technique and his playing with top men – Basie, Gillespie and Herman – he was unable to make a living from music and retired for a couple of years in the summer of 1952. He then joined the Danish-born trombonist Kai Winding to form the Jay and Kay Quintet. Towards the end of the 1950s Johnson turned more to composing and arranging until he became known more widely in that role than as a performer.

MJQ

One of the longest-lived and most widely known modern groups was the Modern Jazz Quartet, which existed from 1952 until 1974. The first MJQ sprang from the Dizzy Gillespie Orchestra and comprised the pianist John Lewis, doyen of modern vibesmen Milt Jackson, drummer Kenny Clarke and bassist Ray Brown. Clarke and Brown were replaced by Connie Kay and Percy Heath a year or so after the formation of the MJQ and, thereafter, the group was stable. The fact that the MJQ was widely recognized outside jazz circles, remained highly popular and was so long lived, says as much for it as for its music. Those who find brass and reeds strident – as many do – will describe the MJQ as 'restful'.

It's certainly easy and pleasant to listen to, swinging and thoughtful music played by fine musicians, but the implied link between 'modern' and 'jazz' in the name seems to me to be questionable.

Charlie Christian

The pioneer bop guitarist was Charlie Christian (1919–42), born in Dallas. He joined Benny Goodman in 1939 and his significant contribution was the use of the electric guitar on which he played virtuoso single-string solos – a technique so common now as to pass unnoticed, but unheard of before Christian. While with Goodman, he fell in with the boppers at Minton's; apart from a new sound, which must have pleased them, he may even have invented the word bebop. Unfortunately, he had precious little time in which to contribute; he contracted tuberculosis in 1941 and died early the following year.

Afterbop

Bop was but the beginning of a new stream of jazz which seemed to be more for musicians than for audiences, until the audiences became accustomed to it. This stream is analogous to modern art of the sort where the artist wishes to express himself, a mandatory part of which is being misunderstood by the public. The public does, eventually, become accustomed to it, by which time, of course, the pioneer artists are well into the next phase but two, and the copyists of their previous styles are well under way.

The players discussed previously were selected from those who founded and popularized the bop/modern jazz stream; there were, of course, scores of others. My final selection moves through the realms of hard bop, cool jazz, free jazz and into uncharted territories. They are presented according to their dates of birth, on the assumption that age may at least have been some determining factor on the point at which they entered the world of jazz and, since we have to stop somewhere, I have taken the final year of birth as 1930. However, before we move into these uncharted territories, we should consider broadly what these musicians were trying to do.

Bop sought to break away from jazz conventions and, in its time, succeeded. It altered the voicing of rhythm, without necessarily making it more complex than jazz had known before. It experimented with new harmonies, which at first sounded 'wrong'. It escaped from simple chord sequences, yet still confined itself within more complex ones. In a comparatively short time, its sounds became familiar – so what could jazz do next?

It exploited its rhythmic element. The drums, which had already broken away from their conventional task of laying down a steady beat, became a front-line instrument and thus took on a very new role. At the same time, the piano was treated more as a percussion instrument so that, instead of the accustomed melodic exchanges between, say, trumpet and sax, we now find rhythmic exchanges between drums and piano.

The pioneer group was named, appropriately enough, the Jazz Messengers; it was formed in 1954 by drummer Art Blakey and pianist Horace Silver – what they played came to be know as hard bop. Silver left Blakey in 1956 to form his own group and developed his brand of hard bop still further by allowing the influence of black church music to act on it: the result was named funky or soul jazz. According to how you look at it, this was either a success or a disaster – it became popular. Certainly, popularity spells success, but equally, if your audience immediately appreciates what you are doing, it may indicate that you're not doing anything new enough!

As a contrast to the driving force of hard bop was cool jazz. The proponent of this style was trumpeter (and flugelhorn player) Miles Davis, and his early experiments – too advanced to be commercially successful – included the distant voice of the French horn and the return of the tuba in a new role. The harmonic writing was such that the fullest sound could be produced with the fewest possible instruments; later, for example, the famed Gerry Mulligan Quartet played without a piano. Cool jazz was not developed as a deliberate contrast to hard bop; Miles Davis's advanced recordings, collected in the album *The Birth of the Cool,* were made in 1949, five years before the formation of the Jazz Messengers.

In free or avant-garde jazz, the music appears to have met developments in the non-jazz world head on and such words as 'atonality' and 'incoherence' are bandied about, according to the views of the people who are bandying. Such music is related not only to the natural experimental development of the art, but also to the expression of political ideas, which has in turn led to misunderstanding and suppression. The complexity of a philosophy wherein suppression of one's chosen art form counts as a political success is beyond me – surely art isn't about that?

Gil Evans

One of the foremost composer/arrangers of the period was Gil Evans (1912–88), born in Toronto. He led his own band through most of the 1930s in Stockton, California; when it was taken over, he continued as its arranger. He spent most of the 1940s with the Claude Thornhill Orchestra, arranging in new and exciting ways – Thornhill used French horns – which, however, went almost entirely unnoticed. As the 1950s dawned, Evans moved into cool jazz with the controversial Miles Davis, Gerry Mulligan and others. He also started to play the piano and tour, which he continued through the 1960s and 1970s, at the same time building up a formidable range of compositions, including much commissioned music.

Pete Rugolo

Born in Sicily in 1915, Pete Rugolo moved to the States in about 1920 and studied music, later under Darius Milhaud; he played jazz piano from his teens. His career turned towards composing and arranging – he was responsible for the sound of the Stan Kenton Orchestra in the second half of the 1940s. After that, he devoted himself almost entirely to composing and directing for record companies, films and TV. He died in 2011.

Art Blakey

Art Blakey (1919–90), born in Pittsburgh, was in the tradition of jazz drummers who were also leaders, having formed his first Jazz Messengers, purveyors of hard bop, in the mid-1950s. Blakey first played with Fletcher Henderson in 1939 and then, after various moves, worked with Billy Eckstine during the existence of the latter's orchestra – that cradle of bop. Blakey drove himself and his colleagues to the limit, giving rise to great excitement for all who could stand the pace.

Lennie Tristano

Born in Chicago, this blind pianist (1919–78) studied music and played in public from an early age. He moved to New York City in the mid-1940s and there founded his Cool School of Jazz, putting his experimental ideas into practice and opening a music school in 1951. From then on, he appeared infrequently in public and made very few recordings, but his ideas were widely promulgated through his pupils and his writings.

Tadd Dameron

A short-lived but essential contributor to bop was the composer/arranger and pianist Tadd Dameron (1917–65), born in Cleveland, Ohio. His association with the Dizzy Gillespie Orchestra in the mid-1940s made him the pioneer big band bop arranger. Towards the end of the 1960s he was imprisoned for a drugs offence, but emerged to write again before ill health overtook him and he finally succumbed to cancer in 1965.

Dave Brubeck

An important and widely known pianist and composer, Dave Brubeck was born into a musical family in Concord (CA) in 1920. He studied music from an early age, through college and with Milhaud and Schoenberg. As well as these studies, he played jazz from his early teens and at the beginning of the 1950s formed his quartet which became world famous through its recordings and tours. Until the mid-1960s the Dave Brubeck Quartet featured the alto player Paul Desmond; at that time, however, Desmond seems to have felt that the directions of modern jazz did not suit him; he left and thereafter kept a low profile. Desmond was to some extent the jazz influence in the quartet: Brubeck himself tended towards a musicians' music, which left many critics uncertain of their reactions. After Desmond's departure, Brubeck's new quartet featured the baritone player Gerry Mulligan. Brubeck has three musical sons – Darius (keyboards, born in 1947), Chris (trombone/bass, born in 1952) and Danny (drums, born in 1955) – and the family maintains its own quartet. Not surprisingly, Brubeck also devoted himself a good deal to composing and moved more and more towards the concert platform in later years. He died in 2012.

Fats Navarro

Trumpeter Fats Navarro (1923–50) was one of the foremost musical originators of his time and, had he lived, it seems clear that he would have been ranked with, and would be as widely known as, Dizzy Gillespie. Navarro was born in Key West, Florida, learned the piano and later the trumpet and was of such calibre that he was able to succeed Dizzy Gillespie, on Gillespie's recommendation, in Billy Eckstine's Band in the mid-1940s. After that, he worked with Illinois Jacquet, Lionel Hampton and Coleman Hawkins and, towards the end of the 1940s, with Tadd Dameron. Sadly drugs and TB took their toll, and he died in 1950.

Sonny Stitt

Born in Boston into a musical family – his father was a professor of music and his brother a concert pianist – Sonny Stitt (1924–82) started on the piano and then studied reeds, especially tenor and alto. He developed his bop style before meeting Charlie Parker, and it must have been somewhat galling to Stitt (if not to Parker) for the two to find that they had arrived at the same musical point independently. Stitt first came to the fore as an original voice with Dizzy Gillespie in the mid-1940s. He went on to record prolifically and tour extensively, latterly with The Giants of Jazz.

Charles Mingus

Best known as a bassist, composer and truly inspiring leader, Charles Mingus (1922–79) was born in Nogales, Arizona, and studied a number of instruments before taking up the bass. He played with a number of bands from the early 1940s, notably those of Louis Armstrong, Kid Ory and Lionel Hampton, with the last of which he established himself as one of the foremost exponents of bop.

Before he became a composer in the mid-1950s, Mingus played with many other pioneers including Charlie Parker and Bud Powell. Some of his compositions were written, but more often he directed from the keyboard, suiting the development of his ideas to the musicians he had at the time, a technique which gave rise to some remarkably exciting performances. Such a driving leader was not always easy to get on with and he had frequent disagreements with both musicians and management. Ill health contributed to his semi-retirement in the mid-1960s, but he returned to the scene in the 1970s and made two European tours.

John Coltrane

John Coltrane (1926–67), a multi-instrumentalist born in Hamlet, North Carolina, played with a number of the foremost modernists from the end of the 1940s – Dizzy Gillespie, Johnny Hodges, Earl Bostic and Miles Davis. In his search for a new direction, he experimented with Indian music in the early 1960s, which led him to a modal approach. He attracted and inspired a number of younger followers, but his health deteriorated and he died in 1967.

Miles Davis

Trumpeter Miles Davis (1926–91) was born in Alton, Ilionois and took up his instrument at the age of 13. At 18, he played in Billy Eckstine's Orchestra with Dizzy Gillespie and Charlic Parker and was soon playing with Parker. In 1948 he studied with Gil Evans and then formed a band with Lee Konitz and Gerry Mulligan which played a cool jazz so far ahead of its time that the band lasted only two weeks.

In the mid-1950s his quintet with John Coltrane pioneered another new direction, but no sooner had he established that than he started to work with young unknowns whom he discovered and developed. Although a critic of those who were further out than he, Davis himself moved towards the use of electronic instruments and effects, and some critics believe that he had said all that he had to say in jazz – which was plenty – by the end of the 1960s.

Oscar Peterson

Through a combination of his musical ability, articulate personality and good management, Oscar Peterson won an enormous audience both within the world of jazz and without it, which has led to unwarranted criticism of his integrity. Peterson was born in Montreal in 1925 and learned the piano from the age of six; in his early teens he won a talent contest and a regular local radio spot. He was 25 before he left Canada to make an outstanding debut at Carnegie Hall, the start of his rise to international fame. He very soon started to work with a trio, at first bass and guitar, the guitar later replaced by drums, but he also worked widely as a soloist, toured with Ella Fitzgerald and made many outstanding duo recordings with other artists. He died in 2007.

Max Roach

One of the greatest drummers of modern jazz, Max Roach (1925–2007) was born in New York City and was early inspired by Kenny Clarke, whose innovations he continued to develop. From the mid-1940s he played with all the greats of bop and its descendants and, in 1954, formed his own quintet which lasted until trumpeter Clifford Brown and pianist Richie Powell – Bud's brother and arranger for the quintet – were killed in a car crash. After this setback, it took him some time to reorganize his group and in the 1960s he fell from favour by introducing some campaigning for racial equality into his compositions. In the 1970s he came to the fore again in new roles, first with the formation of a group of percussion instruments, and second as a teacher – in 1972 he became a professor of music in the University of Massachusetts.

Stan Getz

Another setter of the cool jazz scene was tenorman Stan Getz (1927–91), born in Philadelphia. In the 1940s he was playing with Jack Teagarden, Stan Kenton, Benny Goodman and a Woody Herman Herd. He led his own groups from the 1950s, touring and living abroad extensively. After his contribution to cool jazz, he was largely responsible for the bossa nova craze in the early 1960s, which led him further away from his jazz experiments. Some critics rank Getz as one of the top tenormen of jazz.

Gerry Mulligan

Composer, arranger, baritone saxophonist and sometimes pianist Gerry Mulligan (1927–96) was born in New York City and played with many of the groups we have already met until the end of 1952. Then, in California, he conceived a group without a piano to achieve greater freedom, and with trumpeter Chet Baker the cool, West Coast, Gerry Mulligan Quartet was born. The quartet lived on with various changes of personnel and voices, but its leader continued to work with other groups as well. Mulligan seems to have embraced the whole of the history of jazz, while remaining individually modern.

Horace Silver

Pianist and composer Horace Silver, born in Norwalk, Connecticut in 1928, was first inspired by Bud Powell. In the early 1950s, he played with Stan Getz and was co-founder with Art Blakey of the Jazz Messengers; he then formed his own quintet and developed from hard bop to the foundations of the soul and funky schools, with Latin American influences. Latterly, he became increasingly widely known as a songwriter and has toured the world.

Sonny Rollins

Sonny Rollins was born in New York City in 1930 and, although he was exposed to a musical environment from an early age, came to decide on music as a possible career comparatively late. It was not until the late 1940s that he started to play tenor with the bopmen – Art Blakey, later Bud Powell and Miles Davis, later still Max Roach. In 1957 he started to lead his own groups and soon became bracketed with Stan Getz as a top tenorman. However, he retired from 1959 to 1961 to practise and develop his ideas; then returned to the scene with new vigour to experiment with different presentations – which met with the well-known division of the critics until his ventures came into some musical perspective. He also toured widely until retiring again from 1968 to 1971 for another self-appraisal and self-searching, which included eastern mystical studies. Once again, he returned renewed to compose and tour, playing to an even better understanding by audiences and critics.

Ornette Coleman

Multi-instrumentalist Ornette Coleman was born in Fort Worth, Texas in 1930, taught himself alto then tenor and sax, and was playing R&B around 1950. During that decade he went on to study music part time and emerged with the new concept of free jazz: a form in which all conventional pre-planning is apparently cast aside. This gave rise to sharp controversy among both musicians and critics as to whether at one extreme nothing whatever musical was being said, while at the other that the very freedom of the new music made it (paradoxically) similar to the old. The central view was that musical frontiers were indeed being pushed forward. Coleman continued to experiment, to develop his compositions and to inspire followers; as with Sonny Rollins his ideas have found acceptance among many – there is, perhaps, more resistance from musicians than from an open-minded public.

New Orleans revival

In this chapter you will learn:

► *how Europe discovered jazz*
► *how many retired players rebuilt their jazz careers*
► *how jazz musicians developed 'across the Pond'.*

The development of bop was too much for some ears; whether it sparked off the traditionalist/revivalist movement (returning to the earlier, deemed-to-be-pure jazz) as a protest, or whether that would have happened anyway is difficult to determine. Probably it was just one of a number of factors – the war had ended and Europe had learned a great deal about American culture, notably through films, the radio and the US servicemen stationed in its midst.

Outside America, jazz was not surrounded with the same political and social taboos and thus it was more readily accepted as an art form once the original shock had abated. Between the wars, jazz had begun to develop a life of its own in most parts of the globe according to the availability of films, records, indigenous or visiting musicians and the attitudes of the management of broadcasting companies. Jazz had a message which touched the many who were open to receive it.

Perhaps it is no coincidence that an upsurge of interest in jazz on the east side of the Atlantic coincided with the lifting of the pall of uncertainty and aggression when World War II ended. If an example is needed, consider just one – the Dutch Swing College Band founded by clarinettist Peter Schilperoort (1919–90) in 1945 on the day of liberation.

The world was ready for a revival, and the excitement was enhanced when many of the old musicians were found to be still alive and able to play with varying degrees of proficiency. Oft cited is Bunk Johnson who was researched out of retirement and given some new teeth and a new horn, emerging as a living legend and centrepiece of the revival in 1943. Another old New Orleans musician was George Lewis, a fine clarinettist who suffered a lot of the time from not being told to get in tune. The original tailgate trombonist Edward 'Kid' Ory (1886–1973) completed a New Orleans front line, although the three men didn't stay together for very long. It's worth seeking out records from this period to compare them with those of the earliest – and the latest – jazz.

William Geary 'Bunk' Johnson

One of the most publicized revivalists was the trumpeter (and cornetist) Bunk Johnson (1879–1949), born in New Orleans. He was thus on site for the birth of jazz and claimed that he played with Buddy Bolden from time to time, a possibility denied by clarinettist 'Big Eye' Louis Nelson, who actually did play with Bolden.

However, Johnson's career did not develop in the same way as that of other jazzmen; rather than playing with well-known bands in New Orleans and moving upriver, he toured the vaudeville circuits and by the time he retired from the musical scene in the early 1930s – with neither trumpet nor teeth as the result of a dance-hall fight – was something of a legend. In 1937, he was sought out by the researchers Frederic Ramsey Jr and William Russell; five years later, they provided him with a new trumpet and a new set of teeth (made by Sidney Bechet's dentist brother, Leonard) and he became the centre of the New Orleans revival with Lu Watters' Yerba Buena Jazz Band in San Francisco.

George Lewis

George Lewis (1900–68) was the New Orleans clarinettist who survived for rediscovery at the appropriate time. He taught himself to play the clarinet and from the mid-1910s until the Depression played with numerous bands, including those of Kid Ory and Buddy Petit.

In the 1930s he played less, but was ripe for the New Orleans revival in 1942. After his initial appearances with Bunk Johnson, Lewis formed his own band which toured extensively to mixed receptions. However, when he was in tune, he did produce the sound of the classic New Orleans clarinet (as we know it from records) comparable with that of any other player. He died in his native city in 1968.

Although there were dozens of other musicians associated with the New Orleans revival, those who actually sparked it off are less numerous. Certainly, Johnson and Lewis were of great importance; some of the other musicians whom we have already met were still around to be rediscovered, adapting what they had to offer to meet the commercial needs of the time. And they played to audiences whose interests were different from those of yore: instead of dancing and shouting, they sat in rows, rapt. They had gone to listen to living legends – and it was sometimes difficult to separate the curiosity value from the product itself; one wondered not that it was done well, but that it was done at all. For those who found the modern jazz sounds too much, the familiarity of the old was nostalgic and comforting.

Revival in the UK

Jazz had come a long way in Britain since the visit of the ODJB some 30 years before. In 1923 the Paul Whiteman Orchestra had visited the UK and, whatever the classification of the music he played, Whiteman certainly helped to spread the interest in it. Far removed from Whiteman's symphonic syncopations was the music of the Mound City Blue Blowers, led by the kazoo-playing Red McKenzie, who visited in 1925. No sooner had this sound been assimilated than Whiteman returned for a tour of London and the provinces with a 27-piece orchestra; by this time there was a growing understanding of the differences between Whiteman's music and jazz.

That same year – 1926 – pianist Fred Elizalde (1907–79) formed his Quinquaginta Ramblers in Cambridge (England) and went on to import a number of top American musicians to play at London's Savoy Hotel in 1928 before returning to his native Spain to study music. Elizalde's jazz successor was bassist Spike Hughes (1908–87) who, after leaving the Perse School in Cambridge which, incidentally, also nurtured me and baritone player Ronnie Ross (1933–91), became the foremost name in British jazz of his time and widely known through his recordings for the Decca company (Spike Hughes and his Deccadents) before moving to New York City in 1933, thus reversing the musical trend.

American musicians continued to visit – Louis Armstrong first came in 1933, Duke Ellington the same year, followed by violinist Joe Venuti, pianist Fats Waller (whom my father saw at the Finsbury Park Empire several times in the 1930s) and many others. More often than not, their appearances were at the now defunct music halls throughout the country – such was the status of jazz that they gave music hall (i.e. vaudeville) turns rather than concerts.

Then in 1935 came a disagreement between the British Musicians' Union and the American Federation of Musicians which effectively stopped the British public from hearing live American musicians for some 20 years. American jazz was available on record, via the BBC and in a few films, but if you wanted to hear it live you had to go abroad for it. Meanwhile, British jazz developed through the dance orchestras, a notable advance being the employment of alto and trumpet player Benny Carter (1907–2003) to arrange for the BBC in 1936.

In the 1940s there was a growing interest in jazz in Britain; a new generation of people were discovering it for themselves, a story repeating itself in many other parts of the world. The singer and entertainer George Melly sums it up in his autobiographical volume *Owning Up*. Writing of his schooldays at Stowe:

> One summer evening a friend of mine called Guy Neal, whose opinion I respected, asked me to come and hear a record, it was called 'Eccentric' and was by Muggsy Spanier. Guy explained that the three front-line instruments, trumpet, clarinet and trombone, were all playing different tunes and yet they all fitted together. We listened over and over again until it was dark. I walked across Cobham Court to my dormitory a convert.

> Later that term I was passing an open study window and heard the most beautiful sound in the world. It was Louis Armstrong playing 'Drop That Sack'. I didn't know the boy who owned it, but I knocked on his door and asked if he would play it for me again. I discovered that throughout the school there were little cells of jazz lovers. Slowly I learned something about the music and its history, most of it inaccurate, all of it romantic. I heard my first Bessie Smith record. It was 'Gimme a Pig-foot and a Bottle of Beer'.

All over wartime Britain, at every class level the same thing was happening… Suddenly, as if by some form of spontaneous combustion, the music exploded in all our heads.

And so it was. A little later, I experienced the same excitement myself, organized record sessions at school and was amazed to find how many enthusiastic collectors there were. Some of us got together and started to play ourselves; the same thing was happening up and down the country, and during the 1950s a host of amateur musicians of all sorts was to appear as if from nowhere.

In 1943 at the Red Barn, a pub in Barnehurst, Kent, George Webb's Dixielanders started to play to a growing public and a new phase in British jazz was under way. The Dixielanders' trumpeter was Owen Bryce, whose career in playing and teaching – along with his pianist wife Iris – inspired hundreds and thousands of youngsters (and not so youngsters!) over decades. After Owen Bryce came Humphrey Lyttelton (1921–2008); another cornerstone was Canadian-born clarinettist Wally Fawkes (1924–).

The next landmark was the visit of the Graeme Bell Jazz Band from Australia. Bearing out our theory of the spontaneous generation of jazzbands, Graeme Bell (1914–2012) had formed his in Melbourne in 1943 and had been selected to visit the Prague Youth Festival in Czechoslovakia in 1947. Having been well received there, they decided to pop over to tour England. They started quietly and ended tumultuously; apart from anything else, they encouraged happy jiving as opposed to rapt listening.

The following year, trumpeter Humphrey Lyttelton (ex-George Webb) formed his first band and the voice of George Melly (1926–2007) was first heard in the land.

In 1949 trumpeter Ken Colyer (1928–88) formed what was to become the Crane River Jazz Band. A perfectionist, Colyer visited New Orleans to study the real thing in the early 1950s and returned to lead the outstanding Ken Colyer's Jazzmen, unwavering supporters of Ken's view of the 'true' jazz.

A disagreement in 1954 led to trombonist Chris Barber (1930–) leaving to start his own successful career as a bandleader, supported by trumpeter Pat Halcox (1930–2013) and clarinettist Monty Sunshine (1928–2010), not to mention the extraordinary blues singing of Ottilie Patterson (1932–2011).

The trad boom was at its height. Jazz clubs sprang up in London and the provinces, providing audiences for both local and visiting bands. Names suddenly became well known; some remained so, some sank back to obscurity, some moved out of the trad stream by natural musical evolution, such as Humphrey Lyttelton. Clarinettists were well to the fore: Mister Acker Bilk (1929–), with his hit, 'Stranger on the Shore'; the Sandy Brown (1929–75) in duo with trumpeter Al Fairweather (1927–93); Cy Laurie (1921–2002), an early mystic and cult figure; Terry Lightfoot (1921–2013), a leader from 1954; Monty Sunshine and his famous hit 'Petite Fleur'. Trumpeters not mentioned already include Alan Elsdon (1934–) and the Alex Welsh ((1929–82), the latter noteworthy for turning down an invitation to join Jack Teagarden.

The singer George Melly, originally inspired by Bessie Smith, toured with Mick Mulligan's Magnolia Jazz Band; later writing reviews and critiques during the day and gigging in the evenings as a guest with other bands; later in life with jazz historian and trumpeter John Chilton's Feetwarmers.

These were some of the foremost names of British jazz, many of whom have a wide reputation outside the country; there are hundreds, if not thousands, of other musicians who first took up their instruments at that time and found them impossible to put down again.

In 1955 the musicians' unions sorted out their difficulties and at long last a procession of American jazzmen was able to visit the UK, play to the packed houses which eagerly awaited them and praise many of the home-grown musicians who supported them. Some of the 'living legends' were hardly either; one had to forget the music and bask in the romance of having heard them.

Skiffle etc.

The trad boom was not the only event in British popular music in the late 1940s and 1950s. In the latter decade there was the sudden appearance of skiffle groups, no less happy, perhaps, but from a totally different culture from that of their begetters, the spasm bands of old.

The particular features of the amateur skiffle group were the washboard (some mothers still 'ad 'em) equipped with bells and whistles and played with thimbles, and the tea-chest bass (inverted tea-chest, broom handle and rope). Guitarists usually bought ready-made instruments and there was often a mouth organist (no doubt inspired by Larry Adler's soundtrack for the film *Genevieve* in 1953).

The memorable professional skiffle success was the group formed by banjo/guitarist Lonnie Donegan who hit on a particular formula and made the most of it.

The films *Blackboard Jungle* and *Rock around the Clock* with Bill Haley and His Comets – and the voice of Elvis Presley – hit these shores and a highly copyable formula became intertwined with skiffle and gave rise to the new industry of pop music.

Many of these manifestations had little to do with jazz. The movement gave rise to a lot of less-than-mediocre sound, but it did promote interest in music and performance in general and launched some musicians and entertainers without whom we should be the poorer. And it gave a lot of people a lot of fun.

British modernists

However, perhaps that was a sideline. More important to the jazz scene were the recordings that introduced a new movement called bop, although one wonders how many of its growing following knew what it was about. Two men who *did* take the trouble to find out what was happening were Johnny Dankworth (1927–2010) and Ronnie Scott (1927–96). Reedsmen playing on transatlantic liners, they heard Charlie Parker in New York, came away inspired by what he was doing and translated it into their own terms.

Dankworth formed the Johnny Dankworth 7 in 1950 and his first big band in 1953, two years after featuring the phenomenal singer Cleo Laine, whom he later married. As well as leading his band, Dankworth went on to compose and direct countless film and television scores as one of the UK's most prolific and foremost musicians in the field, and to devote much energy to teaching. Dame Cleo Laine widened her career from singing jazz, but her style has no equal anywhere.

Ronnie Scott formed his own band in 1952. Five years later, with another tenorman, the late Tubby Hayes, he founded the Scott–Hayes Jazz Couriers who purveyed hard bop for some two-and-a-half years. In 1959 he opened his now world-famous Jazz Club, which has built up a substantial reputation over the years as *the* place where visiting musicians appear in London. He himself continued to play until his untimely death in 1996.

Conclusion

We have surveyed about a century of the history and development of jazz and met some of the musicians and bands who played the music in its various styles. Use the information to choose a spectrum of records to clothe the skeleton of words with the flesh of sound.

One point I would stress yet again is that 'old' does not necessarily mean 'old fashioned'. Different streams of evolution coexist. It has caught our fancy that the dinosaurs died out, but the high-profile extinction of the dinosaurs has given the process of evolution a bad press. There are still plenty of large reptile designs which have remained virtually unchanged for millions of years coexisting with the birds that developed from the reptile line. A fish emerged from the sea and spent millions of years producing mammals; then some mammals (whales, dolphins and the like) chose to go back to live in the sea again.

I labour this point because too many people seem to reject ragtime, or New Orleans jazz or 1930s swing, for example, taking the view that they're old fashioned. I want to encourage you to listen to it all; to study the comparative anatomy of all types of jazz and allied music, and see how everything fits together.

Part 2

The structure of jazz

The instruments of jazz

In this chapter you will learn:

▶ *about the instruments traditionally used to play jazz*

▶ *about harmonics*

▶ *about valves.*

When I was very young, I thought of music as a tweety sound that came out of my grandfather's wireless; it was some time before I understood that there were actually people playing instruments to produce that sound. My purpose here is to explain how instruments work and to give you some idea of how they're played – what players have to do to make them *speak*. If you know nothing of this at the moment, the information will help you to understand what you hear and what musicians at live performances are doing – I know from discussion that some non-musicians are a bit vague about this. After meeting the instruments, we will look at the *line-up* – the selection of instruments chosen to make a band.

Brass

CORNET, TRUMPET, TROMBONE, FLUGELHORN, TUBA, SOUSAPHONE

Brass instruments are essentially tubes caused to emit a note when the player purses the lips against the shaped mouthpiece and blows a raspberry into it. This act makes the air in the tube vibrate and produce a sound. The air can be persuaded to vibrate in various modes – slow vibration in one large mass produces the lowest note, and faster vibration in a number of smaller masses produces notes of higher and higher *pitches*. The tension of the player's lips determines the mode of vibration. A series of notes can thus be obtained from a variety of tubes or cavities – animal's horn, conch, bugle, gas pipe, watering can and so on. Why not look around for something suitable and try it? You might even be inspired to take up a brass instrument.

The notes above are the *harmonics* obtainable from a simple pipe about eight feet long – it is, one might say, in the key of C. The 7th*, 11th* and 13th* harmonics sound particularly 'out of tune'. Lengthening such a tube would enable you to play a series of notes lower in pitch; shortening it would raise the pitch of the series.

Harmonics

The reason for the notes becoming closer and closer as they get higher and higher is that the air in the tube vibrates in smaller and smaller 'packets'. When it vibrates in one mass it produces the fundamental note (first harmonic); for the second harmonic the air splits into two masses; for the third harmonic into three and so on. The higher you go up the series, the smaller the difference between the elements of the modes of vibration. For example, the difference between 1/2 and 1/3 (i.e. 1/6) is clearly larger than the difference between 1/9 and 1/10 (1/90).

As you will see, the number of notes is limited, especially towards the lower end of the series; bugle calls are the result of making a virtue of necessity. In order to play the 'missing' notes and produce a complete (chromatic) scale, you need to be able to alter the length of the tube as well as your lip tension. This you do either by adding to or subtracting from the length of the tube by means of *valves* to switch subsidiary lengths in or out (as you find in the cornet or trumpet) or by means of a *slide* (as you find in the slide trombone – there are valve trombones, but they are rarer than the slide variety).

Further modifications to the *pitch* (highness or lowness) and *timbre* (quality) of the sound may be obtained by controlling the lips and tongue and using trick fingering and *mutes*. Some mutes are designed to plug into the end of the instrument and give a strangulated sound, or are manipulated for a 'wah-wah' sound; others are makeshift items such as hats, beer mugs, buckets and sink plungers. Some jazz brass players from King Oliver onwards have been particularly famed for their work with mutes.

The trumpet and cornet differ in appearance (the cornet is chunkier) but play in the same range. The flugelhorn is a larger and richer instrument which came into jazz use more recently. In the lower voices, there are the trombone, the tuba (a larger and therefore deeper-voiced instrument) and the lowest-pitched of all, the sousaphone. This last, the 'brass bass' (as opposed to the string bass), encircles the player; originally its *bell* (wide end) pointed towards the sky, but nowadays it is arranged to point forward. All these instruments, with the exception of the slide trombone, have three valves to alter the pitch of the note. Valve trombones are sometimes seen.

Valves

Instruments of the trumpet family have three valves, usually plungers (sometimes rotary), which move against a spring when depressed with the fingers and control the length of tube in play. Because the rising harmonics of the open tube become closer and closer, there is less valve manipulation and more adjustment to the embouchure when you are playing higher passages.

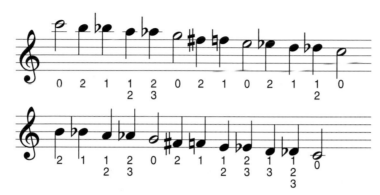

Valve positions for playing a chromatic scale on the trumpet

Those familiar with binary arithmetic will instantly see that three valves allow for eight possible combinations: 000 (all valves released), 001, 010, 011, 100, 101, 110 and 111 (all valves depressed). However, reference to the example shows that valve three is never used alone; we thus have to think of seven combinations.

Not surprisingly, we find that the trombone has seven slide positions; it is up to the player to find each one accurately. Playing the slide trombone therefore requires both a good ear and a good kinaesthetic sense. Because the natural harmonics are more widely spaced at the lower end of its register, slide trombone work is more spectacular down there. The ability to play *glissando* – a note of constantly changing pitch as the trombonist moves the slide – should be used sparingly, and the possibility of using the foot to move the slide (*à la* George Brunis) should be quickly forgotten.

Reeds

CLARINET, BASS CLARINET, SAXOPHONE FAMILY

Another way of causing the air in a tube to vibrate, and hence produce a note, is to blow through a mouthpiece – a shaped fixed tube fitted with a *reed* (a flexible tongue of bamboo or plastic tapering in thickness) able to vibrate against it.

This is the principle of the clarinet (the first reed instrument of jazz), the bass clarinet (a less used, but nevertheless sweet-sounding instrument) and the saxophone (sax) family: sopranino, soprano, alto,

C-melody, tenor, baritone and bass. Among instruments on which jazz is commonly played, the clarinet and some soprano saxes are straight tubes; all the rest are curved to accommodate their lengths. The clarinet is a generally parallel-sided tube; the tubes of the saxophones are tapered.

The saxophone family

The saxophone family was invented and developed by Adolphe (Antoine-Joseph) Sax (1814–94), a Belgian by birth. His father, Charles Sax, was a maker of wind instruments. Young Adolphe studied the clarinet at the Brussels Conservatoire and was inspired to produce improvements to the instrument and to build his first 'saxophones'. He moved to Paris in 1842 and his saxhorn (patented in 1845) was quickly taken up by French military bands, upsetting the instrument makers of Paris who tried to put Sax out of business. Sax patented the saxophone in 1846, but it was little used outside France until the end of the nineteenth century. It somehow became associated with jazz in about 1915 and since then has become identified with jazz more than any other instrument – especially in the ears of adverse critics. The reason probably lies in the tone of the saxophone; according to the competence of the player, it is capable of a wide range of expression and its ability to play in the manner of the human voice makes it sympathetic to the spirit of the music.

Adam Carse wrote in 1939: 'When it became popular as a dance-band instrument the saxophone lost status and dignity and a style of playing developed which was mercifully never known to the originator.' However, I would venture to suggest that Adolphe Sax, since he saw fit to design an instrument that sounded like that, would be delighted by its contribution to jazz, by its virtuosity and by the pleasure which his invention has given to so many people, both players and listeners.

The notes produced by these instruments are altered by opening and closing holes along the tube. Since we have a limited number of fingers and a limited stretch, intricate keywork is provided to promote musical agility. The range of the instrument is further increased by a *speaker*, or *octave vent*, a hole which, according to whether it is open or shut, determines whether the instrument plays in its high or low *register*.

The lower register of the clarinet is called the *chalumeau* after the much older instrument without a higher register from which the clarinet developed. Johnny Dodds played wonderful chalumeau.

As listeners to jazz will soon realize, the tone of a reed instrument is very much under the control of the player. It is variable according to the material of which the instrument is made, the design of the mouthpiece, the material and *lay* of the reed (the way the reed relates to the body of the mouthpiece) and the *embouchure* – the way the player sets the mouth to the instrument. When we compare the range of these variations with those acceptable in a non-jazz player, we at once appreciate an essential quality of jazz freedom.

The oboe and bassoon have double reeds, which vibrate one against the other. They have occasionally been used in jazz, but are not generally thought of as jazz instruments.

Other wind instruments

Passing quickly by serpents, ophicleides and other instruments seldom found in jazz bands, we reach others wherein the air in a tube is caused to vibrate by blowing *across* it. First, there is the piccolo (important in marching bands) and flute family; since amplification became available the flute has found more favour as a jazz instrument. Second, there are instruments with penny whistle-type mouthpieces, including the recorder family and the Swannee whistle – a tube with a sliding piston within it to change the note, effectively used as a novelty instrument on occasions.

Strings

VIOLIN, DOUBLE BASS, GUITAR, BANJO

In the string family, the sound is produced by a vibrating string and amplified by the construction of the body of the instrument, if not by electronic means. The string is caused to vibrate by bowing, plucking or striking it. Of the orchestral instruments, jazz rarely uses other than the violin and the double bass.

The violin is usually bowed rather than plucked and it is interesting that there are few very good jazz violinists, With most other instruments, there are players with a whole range of abilities; the violin seems (fortunately) to be played well or not at all.

The double bass, at least in the old days, was usually plucked rather than bowed, the sharp *attack* of the string being released being more audible (without it necessarily having to smack the fingerboard); later players produced some very fine bowed playing. The double bass is also capable of novelty effects such as slapping, which have their place if not overused. Spinning the bass on its spike has nothing to do with music of any sort – it's just a bit of *joie de vivre*.

The note produced by a string depends on its tension, mass and length. A slacker, heavier, longer string vibrates more slowly and hence produces a lower note than a tighter, lighter, shorter string. Have a look inside a piano. At the bass end, strings are slack, long and heavily overwound to increase their mass per unit length. The very lowest come in ones, because they can produce a lot of noise. To compete in volume, higher strings come in pairs and, a couple of octaves or so above that, strings come in threes. At the top end, strings are very tight, very light, very short. An *open* string is tuned by adjusting its tension in order to produce the desired note. The only quantity which it is convenient to change while playing is length, and the strings can be *stopped* at desired lengths by pressing them against a *fingerboard* (with the fingers). The construction of the instrument is such that any note is obtainable within the designed range of the string since it can be stopped anywhere along that range.

Guitar tuning

The most usual tuning for the guitar, *always* used by classical players, is standard tuning:

There is, of course, an almost infinite number of tunings, with different types of strings (single or overwound) being available in any position. In practice, only about 100 (!) tunings are used. The most usual are dropped (or lowered) D tuning (example *a*), dropped (or lowered) G tuning (example *b*), and open G (or slack key, Spanish, Hawaiian or Sebastopol) tuning (example *c*):

a   b   c

12-String Guitar

A guitar normally has six strings, but these are sometimes doubled up (six pairs make a 12-string guitar) to give a full, rich tone such as is heard from Leadbelly.

There are various ways of tuning the 12-string guitar but the most usual is for the top three pairs (E, B, G) to be tuned in *unison* (to the same note) and the bottom three pairs (D, A, E) to be tuned an octave apart (one 'normal'; the other an octave above):

Such freedom is not the case with the guitar and banjo (ukulele, mandolin, etc.) which have transverse metal *frets* on their fingerboards so that the strings are, perforce, stopped at those fixed points. Some variation in the note produced may be obtained by pushing the strings sideways and thus increasing the tension (and raising the note); in the electric guitar, variations may be obtained by varying the tension of the strings with a lever (wobble, wobble).

The Spanish guitar uses gut or nylon strings which produce a more mellow tone than the steel strings more often used on other instruments. The strings are plucked either with the fingers and thumb or with a *plectrum* (or *plectra*). Both the material of the plectrum and the position of plucking affect the tone of the note the instrument produces.

Another effect is obtained with *bottleneck* playing; a ring such as the neck of a bottle is placed on the little finger of the left hand, producing a tone similar to that of an Hawaiian guitar, such as we hear from Muddy Waters.

The construction and playing of the guitar-type instruments differ from those of the violin family in that the former are designed to produce chords of up to as many notes as the instrument has strings. Playing more than one string on the violin is possible and often done; on the double bass it is far less usual. It all depends on the dexterity (or perhaps I should say sinistrality) of the performer.

Plucking a steel string produces a very powerful attack on the note produced and guitars have benefited greatly (even if audiences have not) from the development of amplifiers capable of reproducing the sound of the instrument without distortion. (Although it has to be said that sometimes distortion is the least of anyone's worries.)

Electronics and music

An amplifier for the guitar, and for the vocalist, was perfectly in order – indeed, it enabled both to compete on equal terms with the rest of the musicians and promoted some excellent performers without whom our lives would be the poorer – but amplification gradually took over as every instrument demanded its microphone and the sound levels had to be turned up and up as all the players competed. The development of the transistor in the 1950s led to more compact, powerful amplifiers that were low in distortion. This was directly responsible for the emergence of the new pop scene in the mid-50s born out of the rock 'n' roll craze, popularized initially by Bill Haley and His Comets who provided the music for 'The Blackboard Jungle' (1955) and the following year 'Rock around the Clock'. Audiences began to demand that bands become louder and louder until permanent hearing damage set in, although there is some evidence that the damage is less if one is 'enjoying' the noise. Thumping rhythm gradually supplanted tunes, which died out because nobody could hear them. When rhythm is all and it matches the natural frequency of your body, it acts as a powerful physical strobe and may have a similarly devastating effect as that of a strobe light.

The guitar and banjo have always played versatile roles: as solo or band instruments and, if in the band, either as front-line or rhythm section instruments. The banjo solo and that fine sound, the banjo orchestra, were features of minstrel shows and were carried into jazz bands because the instrument has a sharp attack and thus a voice which can be heard in concert with the other instruments – moreover, that quality was an advantage in the days of acoustic recording. The guitar accompanying a blues singer is commonplace; the guitar has a much more singing quality than the banjo and is therefore more suited to accompanying the voice. In jazz bands, the guitar has emerged comparatively recently: amplified, it was first exploited by Charlie Christian who joined Benny Goodman in 1939; sadly, he did not live to develop and benefit from the technique which others so readily took up.

The electric bass guitar is now often used as a substitute for the double bass, compared with which it has both advantages and disadvantages. Its capabilities and techniques are different in that it has frets; it is more portable, although it needs its associated amplifiers and speakers, so this is an advantage only if it is competing with other amplified instruments when such ancillary equipment is needed anyway.

Percussion

Apart from the drum kit, to which we will return in a moment, percussion includes tuned instruments such as the marimba, xylophone, vibraphone (vibes) and the tuned oil drum of the steel band, all of which produce distinctive and sweet sounds. Vibes are the most commonly used in jazz and were introduced sparingly in the 1930s by Red Norvo and Lionel Hampton; one of the best-known exponents is Milt Jackson, late of the Modern Jazz Quartet.

The drummer, like the bassist, has seen a marked change in the role over the last few decades. Originally, the drums were there to provide a steady beat, with cross-rhythms according to the skill and taste of the performer. The drummer was sometimes given a solo in order to demonstrate the art, again according to skill and taste, but remained firmly in the rhythm section. Once the drummer had proved his prowess as a solo instrumentalist (would a woman behave like this?), there would often be a feature number when he would be left alone on the stage while the rest of the band ostentatiously trooped off to the bar for half an hour and then even more ostentatiously trooped back to take up their instruments and blow a final frenzied chorus; crowd pleasing that could reach the height of tastelessness. Later, the drums sometimes played the role of a front-line instrument, taking part in thoughtful and complex exchanges with other front-line instruments; some bands have been led by drummers.

The items in a drum kit are many and vary according to the style of the player. The staple diet is the *bass drum* operated with a pedal, the *hi-hat* cymbal operated with another pedal and the *snare* drum (a wire snare vibrates against its lower skin to give it its characteristic sound), all borrowed and adapted from marching band practice. The snare drum, and other pieces in the kit are usually played with sticks or wire brushes. There may also be a selection of other cymbals, sometimes with rivets around the edges to give a distinctive ring, tom-toms, wood blocks, cow bells and skulls. The last three are usually rejected by modern drummers as 'old fashioned'; the story is that they were introduced into the drum kit to obviate the shortcomings of acoustic recording, since their percussive characteristics are well suited to direct record cutting by mechanical means.

The vibraphone

The vibraphone has aluminium alloy chime bars suspended on elastic cords and arranged in two ranks in a layout similar to that of the piano keyboard. The sound is amplified by a tuned tubular resonator mounted beneath each bar and a vibrato is imparted to it by motorized rotating fans. The fan feature gives the instrument its name; its speed of rotation varies the rate of the vibrato. The player may use two (or even more) hammers in each hand.

Although the principle of drumming is obvious, the role of the drummer in the band is crucial and not as easy as it appears at first sight. Nothing can upset a band more than an arrhythmic drummer.

PSPG

Mechanical music tends to be just that. The contemporary American composer Steve Reich, born in 1936, built his PSPG (phase-shifting pulse gate) to demonstrate that his music is not as mechanical as is sometimes supposed. Thinking once that it might be fun to have my own rhythm section, I tried a keyboard on approval, but took it back for a refund after a couple of days because of the inflexibility of its rhythm generator. I later acquired a more upmarket keyboard with over a hundred different rhythm settings, each with parts A and B and with intro and outro sections. A block of rhythms was listed for piano accompaniment. These didn't work, so I took the keyboard to the local approved service station where they downloaded new software for it. It still didn't work, so they sent it back to the manufacturer, who eventually returned it and confessed that that particular model didn't have that block of rhythms. *'Twas on a Monday morning...*

Keyboards

Our final selection for the band is from instruments played with keyboards, of which the most important during the emergence of jazz was the piano. Today, the term 'keyboards' embraces the conventional piano, the organ, the electric piano and other electronic marvels providing a variety of built-in voices and rhythms – not to mention means of recording – which, carried to the extreme, obviate the need for a performer. The word 'keyboards' is used both generically (anything with a keyboard) and specifically (a keyboard instrument which doesn't have another name, such as piano, harpsichord, etc.).

In their favour, it must be said that many keyboards are lighter and occupy less space than a 'proper' piano and have helped to introduce to music a lot of people who might never otherwise have had such an opportunity. (Here speaks someone who likes his full seven octaves *and* an opportunity to see the action at work.) Contrariwise, the finest keyboards are as cumbersome to lug about as a real piano.

The piano has always been an ambivalent instrument, in that it is sometimes part of the rhythm section, sometimes part of the front line. The piano is one of the few instruments capable of being played solo for any length of time without becoming wearisome and certainly the only one which can produce ten – or even more – notes at a time. That said, however, its notes are immutably fixed by the construction and tuning of the instrument and in that respect it is more limited than many others.

The village hall piano

Pianists are the only musicians who do not carry their instruments about with them, stoically bearing the derisive cries of their fellow musicians (save, perhaps, the string bassist), never knowing what instrument the organizers of the gig are going to provide – if, indeed, they remember to provide one at all. Generally, if the pianist turns up and finds that there's no piano, he (I use that pronoun advisedly) stays around and props up the bar, if only because he's given half the band a lift so he'll have to stay to the bitter end.

A pianist's worst fear is the non-overstrung, wood-framed instrument with broken keys smeared with something sticky and unpleasant. First, remove the *top door* (i.e. what you shouldn't call the front), the *bottom door* and the *fall* (i.e. what you shouldn't call the lid) and remove superfluous and foreign matter such as the broken hammers, strings, coins between the keys, feathers and things to return to the kitchen.

Reset the pedals and the dampers. Then see whether the instrument is plausibly in tune with itself and then what relationship (if any) it has to the other instruments of the band. If you're lucky, the front-line instruments may be able to meet your tuning. It is at this point that someone will claim that the accuracy is 'good enough for jazz', someone else will say 'What do you mean, get in tune? I tuned it last week' or 'Here, I've only just bought it'. There's no stopping it.

If tuning is difficult, you may find yourself struggling to play in unfamiliar keys. If tuning is impossible, you can abandon ship and go and read the latest copy of *New Scientist* (that's the sort of thing pianists do), but don't forget to reassemble the piano first – the caretaker won't have a clue.

The piano has always been a popular instrument in the home, not least because of its ability to make music at the hands of one performer. The piano was – and is – an instrument widely taught and learned, with an enormous repertoire of written music of all sorts. It is no accident that many composers, arrangers and bandleaders were – and are – pianists. When you come to think of it, no other instrument displays its range of notes, speaks at the touch of a single finger *and* acts as a writing desk.

The use of the harpsichord, harmonium or organ in jazz has generally been more of a novelty than an advance in the art. More recently, electronic keyboards have come into their own and introduced the possibility of effects to be exploited both in jazz and in other popular music. They have the advantage of freeing the player from the horrors of the village hall piano; moreover, since most bands nowadays have amplification equipment, the keyboard can simply be plugged in along with everything else.

The jazz band line-up

Our survey of musical instruments explains how the instruments of jazz work and gives some idea of how they are used. I want to help you to understand why the music sounds as it does – and perhaps even inspire you to start playing. If anyone feels very strongly about some esoteric instrument on which some artist once played a jazz solo which I've forgotten to mention, I apologize now.

Many people who want to make music choose a particular instrument because it happens to be handy. This certainly happened in the early days of jazz and it is no coincidence that the usual instruments of jazz were those found in military bands – trumpets, cornets, clarinets, trombones, drums – and readily available to aspiring musicians, some of whom might join the army for tuition and perhaps security.

I have already used the terms *front-line* and *rhythm section* instruments and the meanings are probably self-explanatory – the front-line players stand at the front of the band and play the melody and its harmonic accompaniment, and members of the rhythm section sit or stand at the back and play the rhythm accompaniment.

In the front line we may find trumpet or cornet, clarinet, sax(es) and trombone; that such instruments are there is, of course, no accident, for they are instruments with loud and complementary voices. The role of the trumpet (or cornet) – that of playing the melody while the trombone and clarinet provide the lower and higher voices respectively – is clearly crucial, so more often than not the trumpeter (or cornettist) was (and is) the leader of the band.

The rhythm section comprises drums, (brass, later string, later still electric) bass, banjo (later guitar), sometimes piano. With the exception of the piano, these are all instruments of marching, minstrel or spasm bands.

The vibes, like the violin, tends to be a front-line instrument since, if it is played at all, it must be played well and is therefore *featured*.

We have now gathered what we might call a conventional – or traditional? – jazz band of some six or seven players, the reasons for its line-up being both accidental (because of the availability of the instruments) and practical (because of the complementary natures of their voices). Let's go on to look at the structure of the music we might play with such a band.

Rudiments of music

In this chapter you will learn:

▶ *the basics of music*
▶ *about the musical structure of jazz.*

Introduction

This section is designed to give you some understanding of music and the musical structure of jazz. I'm applying the principle that knowing how the car works makes you a more understanding (but not necessarily a better) driver. In this case, you may find that you have enough information to be able to build cars of your own.

Some of the terms and concepts I introduce may seem complex, but most of them are well known to jazz musicians – even if they've never seen them introduced in such a full and logical way as they are here! I have found that many jazz musicians know more about some aspects of musical theory than do many non-jazz players, and they toss technical terms about without thinking.

As you will see, my approach encourages you to think of music in terms of patterns – a meeting of aesthetics and arithmetic – and it's no coincidence that those attracted to jazz seem to be on the science, rather than on the arts, side. When I played in bands in the Cambridge area in the days of the jazz revival of the fifties and sixties, almost all the jazz musicians I knew were scientists, engineers and mathematicians.

(For an extremely helpful book on musical theory – designed to help you to pass Grade 5 Theory with little sweat – I commend *Take Five* by Chris Dunn, distributed by Music Sales Ltd and obtainable from your music shop or from Amazon etc.)

Chords and dots

You are no doubt familiar with the appearance of conventional music – the 'dots'. Most jazz musicians – especially those who play the older types of jazz – play from chords and carry a chord book. Those with an interest in rhyming slang sometimes refer to 'the Norfolks' ('Norfolk Broads' = chords).

If you are able to play a musical instrument – particularly one with a keyboard – but know little of music from the chordal point of view, the following exposition may well give you a different outlook on the way tunes are constructed. If you don't play an instrument, this section will give you an insight into the patterns of music and the way jazz is presented and may even inspire you to become a player. There's enough information here to enable you to get started on a keyboard.

Chord symbols are a different and less constraining (or less precise, according to how you look at it) way of conveying the tradition or the intentions of the composer to the player. This section explains all, and if you work through it diligently you should be able to approach any tune without fear.

I'm concentrating on describing music from a chordal point of view, because that is the best way of thinking about jazz. However, I don't want to throw away the dots altogether, for conventional musical notation is an indispensable shorthand for showing how a tune 'goes' and how the melody and its rhythm relate to its chordal structure. If you are coming to music fresh, you need to know something about the dots. If you know about dots already, that knowledge will help you to come to terms with the chords.

I should mention the importance and value of singing. Singing helps you to understand a tune and you may even be able to hear the accompanying harmonies in your head. Remember – if you can't sing it, you can't play it.

Remember, if you play from the dots, you cannot do other than play the same thing over and over again. If you use the dots as a guide to the tune and understand the chordal structure thoroughly, you will immediately feel musical freedom engulf you.

Books with titles such as *100 Great Popular Songs of the Twenties* provide you with the melody and accompanying chords for each tune and sometimes the words as well.

Reading a single line of music isn't all that difficult – find out which note to start on and then see whether subsequent notes go up or down and by how much.

The keyboard

I suggest that, if possible, you have to hand a keyboard of some sort but preferably not an accordion! (Not that I have anything against accordions – it's just that they're rather unwieldy if you're trying to read a book with one hand and work them with the other, especially if you want to see what you're doing.) A keyboard wears its heart on its sleeve, as it were – you can see the notes and their patterns in a way that other instruments deny you. The simplest electronic keyboard is better than nothing, but it must be able to play several notes simultaneously.

Track 9

▶ **The great stave**

Let's see how the dots represent musical notes. By convention, the *great stave* (or great staff) consists of 11 lines, a note on the sixth line representing *middle C*, which takes its name from its position on the piano keyboard.

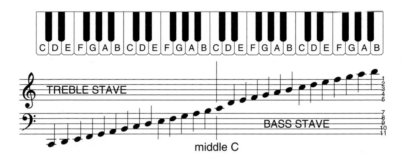

To make the layout easier to read, the sixth line is left out; a fragment of it appears when needed (as with middle C). A note below the 11th line represents F an octave and a half below middle C, and a note sitting on the top line represents G an octave and a half above middle C. The limits are extended by the use of *ledger lines* to extend the staves and *transposing* higher notes into lower registers or vice versa.

A curly ampersand-like symbol – the *treble clef* – denotes that a particular stave is the upper one; alternatively, the *bass clef* denotes the lower one. This is particularly important if you're presented with one stave only.

The figure shows the repeating pattern of the keyboard and the way it relates to the dots. The white notes are designated by the letters A to G. The names of the black notes are related to those of their adjacent white notes; a black note is either the sharp (#) of the note below it or the flat (♭) of the note above it, according to the context. The 'natural' symbol (♮) indicates that a note has reverted to what it was before it was sharpened or flattened.

If we choose a note and play adjacent notes from it up or down the keyboard, we find that there are seven white and five black ones before we arrive at a note with the same name as that from which we started. The *interval* between our starting and finishing notes is called an *octave* (because there are eight notes in a scale) and the interval between any two adjacent notes is a *semitone*. The interval between a note and the next but one is a *whole tone* or simply a *tone*.

◀)) ▶ **The time signature**

Track 10 The forms of the dots also indicate how long a note lasts when it is sounded; how the rhythm of the tune fits into the beats in each of the *bars* into which the tune is divided. At the beginning of each piece of music is a *time signature*, telling you how many of which sort of note fit into a bar. By far the most common for our purposes is '4/4 time'. This is indicated at the beginning of the piece in one of two ways, shown in Example 1. The 'C' is a medieval relic, now taken to mean 'common' (i.e. 4/4) time.

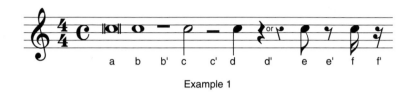

Example 1

The unit of musical time is the semibreve or whole note (as they say in the States), written as a tail-less egg (b). (The breve (a) doesn't get much of a look in unless you're a church organist trying to triturate the congregation with a 64-foot pedal note.)

A semibreve is two minims or half notes (c), four crotchets or quarter-notes (d), eight quavers or eighth-notes (e), 16 semiquavers or sixteenth-notes (f) and so on.

We also need a means for indicating that nothing is happening and the symbols for equivalent rests are shown at b', c', d', e' and f'.

A 4/4 time signature means that each bar contains four quarter-notes (or any combination of notes and rests whose values add up to four quarter notes). Here are some examples of notes and rests adding up to four quarters; a dot after a note makes it half as long again.

Note that notes of the same values may be joined by *beams* so that we write (b) rather than (a).

(a)   (b)

Listening

The salad days story draws attention once again to the importance of *listening*. Listen to records, not to learn the solos note by note, but to get to know the tunes and understand the structure of jazz and the way the performers work together. Sing along with the records (depending on who else is present) to enhance the experience. Attend live performances and study what's going on within the band – the signals members make to one another, arrangements developed on the hoof, the way someone makes a musical statement and others pick it up and run with it.

Sitting in

When you feel confident enough – and I realize it takes not a little confidence – ask if you may *sit in* with a band that plays the sort of music with which you're familiar. Most bands welcome the occasional sitter in and will let you choose your favourite tune, support you in your efforts and congratulate you afterwards. Just don't get carried away; if they want you to play another, they'll ask you. If they don't, it doesn't mean they don't like you; just that they have a job to do and want to stick with their tried way of doing it.

17

Scales and chords

In this chapter you will learn:

- ▶ *about scales*
- ▶ *about chords*
- ▶ *about key signatures*
- ▶ *about the names of notes and intervals.*

Scales

So, back to the keyboard. Let's have a look at some scales: start on middle C and play all the white notes up to the next C (indicated by C') – C D E F G A B C' (below). (Don't ask me why the letters A–G are attached to the notes in the way they are, but if you find out please let me know.) You have just played a scale in the key of C major and you should find its sound familiar. (If you don't, we may have a bit of a problem.)

Count the number of notes – C 1, D 2, E 3, F 4, G 5, A 6, B 7, C' 8 – eight notes; that's why the distance between the end notes is called an *octave*. Play the scale again, looking at the keyboard pattern. You can, if you wish, think of a rising scale as 'take a note (K, the keynote), play the next tone (T), the next tone (T), the next semitone (S), tone (T), tone (T), tone (T), semitone (S)'. Remember this pattern – T, T, S, T, T, T, S – and you'll be able to play a scale starting on any note.

Each group of four notes (in this case C D E F and G A B C') is called a *tetrachord* (which means a group of four notes in progression). A scale consists of first and second tetrachords (T_1 and T_2).

The scale of C you have just played, familiar to our western ears, is the only *diatonic* (from a Greek root meaning 'stretched') scale you can play purely on white notes. If you play all adjacent notes (... SSSSSSSSSS ...), you're playing a *chromatic* scale (*khroma* = colour).

If you wish to start on any white note other than C, you will have to introduce one or more sharps or flats (black notes) in order to produce the same effect (TTSTTTS). Take the second tetrachord of the C scale – G A B C. You will hear that those notes are the first tetrachord of the scale of G: G A B C – completed by D E F# G (example A). The second tetrachord of the scale of G is also the first of the scale of D: D E F# G, completed by A B C# D (example B). If you're not using a keyboard to follow this, I urge you to do so.

Example A

Example B

You will see the pattern emerging (refer to Table 1 for the full set of scales). Remember that the scale of C has no sharps or flats. You will see that the scale of G has one sharp (F#), the scale of D has two (F# and C#) and so on until we get to the scale of F# (which may equally well be thought of as G♭). From then on, we think of the scales as being in flat keys and the number of flats is reduced by one every step (which is, of course, equivalent to getting sharper).

Table 1 The 12 diatonic scales

| Key | Notes of scale – | | #s or ♭s |
	1st tetrachord	2nd tetrachord	
C	C D E F	G A B C	No #s or ♭s
G	G A B C	D E F# G	1 #
D	D E F# G	A B C# D	2 #s
A	A B C# D	E F# G# A	3 #s
E	E F# G# A	B C# D# E	4 #s
B	B C# D# E	F# G# A# B	5 #s
{F#	F# G# A# B	C# D# F F#	6 #s} *
G♭	G♭ A♭ B♭ B	D♭ E♭ F G♭	6 ♭s
D♭	D♭ E♭ F G♭	A♭ B♭ C D♭	5 ♭s
A♭	A♭ B♭ C D♭	E♭ F G A♭	4 ♭s
E♭	E♭ F G A♭	B♭ C D E♭	3 ♭s
B♭	B♭ C D E♭	F G A B♭	2 ♭s
F	F G A B♭	C D E F	1 ♭
C'	C D E F	G A B C	No #s or ♭s

*We tend to use sharps when the keys are moving towards the halfway scale of F# and flats when they're moving away from it. Call it F# or G♭ – it's a matter of taste or how the dots fall best if you're writing them on the stave.

Key signatures

Track 12

Music could be written on the staves as shown in the examples just given. However, knowing the key helps the player to understand the 'feel' of the music, and music in any given key tends to use the notes of the diatonic scale of that key. To save peppering the page with sharps and flats, each key therefore has a key signature as follows:

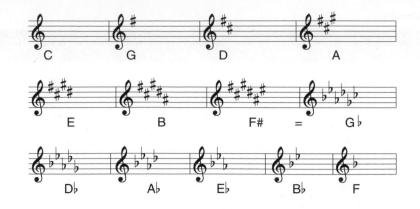

There's a *key signature* at the beginning of each piece of music and another whenever there's a sustained key change within the piece. The key signature reflects the number and positions of the sharps or flats in the scale of the key in which the music is written.

The naming of notes

Track 13

Table 1 gave the eight notes of each of the 12 scales. Now we need to look at naming systems which describe the relative positions of the notes in scales irrespective of the key.

I have already mentioned the idea of *intervals* – the distance between notes. We have met the semitone, the tone and the octave. Table 2 shows the notes 1–8 of any diatonic scale and the names of the intervals between the keynote and the other notes.

In practice, we can omit the words 'major' and 'perfect' without ambiguity – with one exception to which I will return later in the book: the 7th.

Table 2 gives part of the story; you will find names for the 'in between' intervals in Table 3.

Table 2 Diatonic intervals

Note of diatonic scale	Interval from keynote
1	—
2	Major 2nd
3	Major 3rd
4	Perfect 4th
5	Perfect 5th
6	Major 6th
7	Major 7th
8	Perfect 8th (octave)

Table 3 Diatonic and chromatic intervals

Number of note of chromatic scale – number of semitones from keynote	Name of diatonic interval (as in Table 2)	Name of chromatic interval
0	—	—
1		Minor 2nd
2	Major 2nd	
3		Minor 3rd
4	Major 3rd	
5	Perfect 4th	
6		Augmented 4th or diminished 5th
7	Perfect 5th	
8		Augmented 5th or minor 6th
9	Major 6th	
10		Augmented 6th or minor 7th
11	Major 7th	
12	Octave	

The words 'minor' and 'diminished' have precise musical meanings into which we don't need to delve. They are sometimes replaced by the word 'flattened' – which is an equally good description in this context.

We are beginning to delve into areas of less relevance, but I need to introduce a further set of names for the notes of the diatonic scale because jazz (and other) musicians use them, so you should meet the vocabulary to avoid being nonplussed (see Table 4).

Table 4 Relative positions of notes in scale

Note of diatonic scale	Name of position of note in scale	Interval from keynote
1	Tonic or keynote	—
2	Supertonic (above the tonic)	Major 2nd
3	Mediant (midway between tonic and dominant)	Major 3rd
4	Subdominant (below the dominant)	Perfect 4th
5	Dominant	Perfect 5th
6	Submediant (between subdominant and octave)	Major 6th
7	Leading note	Major 7th
8	Octave	Perfect 8th (octave)

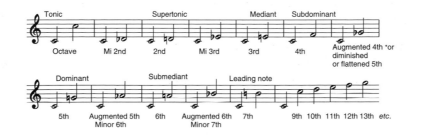

Musical summary of Tables 2, 3 and 4.

The fifth

One of the most important intervals – perhaps *the* most important – is the fifth. Not for nothing is it called the dominant. Those who tune instruments use that characteristic sound of two notes a fifth apart to check and adjust the tuning. If you look back at the table of scales, you will see that they progress by fifths; the second tetrachord (by definition) begins on the fifth note of the scale. The piano tuner tunes by fifths, coming down an octave from time to time to keep within the confines of the middle octaves of the keyboard until he or she has brought in every note:

Why has the fifth such a characteristic sound? Sound is caused by vibration; in the case of the piano, by the vibration of the strings. A note is characterized by the number of vibrations it makes in one second – the unit is the Hertz (one cycle per second = 1Hz). The International Standard for tuning is an A that vibrates at 440 Hz, known as A440. The fifth above that A – that is to say E – vibrates at 660Hz – 1.5 times faster. That simple ratio (2:3) causes a characteristically pleasing sensation when it reaches your ear.

If you refer to the diagram showing the harmonics of the simple tube, you will see that it is no coincidence that the notes sounded by the 2nd and 3rd are a 5th apart (C–E) as are the 4th and 6th (another C–E), 6th and 9th (G–D), 8th and 12th (yet another C–E) and 10th and 15th (E–B). The numbers of these harmonics are all in the ratio 2:3.

Equal temperament

I will mention – just this once – the complex subject of 'temperament': the fine-tuning required particularly by keyboard instruments (because the player cannot adjust the pitch of the note played). Suffice it to say that everything is not as neat as it seems in that, as your tuning progresses, you will find that some of the notes in one scale are not quite right for other scales and have to be adjusted. So, for example, the pitch of E as the third note of the scale of C is not quite the same as the pitch of E as the fifth note of the scale of A. And this is only one example – the same argument applies to each note of the keyboard in relation to some of the others.

Some early keyboard experimenters provided split keys so that, for example, you could play one of the Es when playing in C and the other when playing in A, but it gets very complicated when you try to temper the whole keyboard.

The answer, as always, lies in arithmetic and as long ago as 1636 the French mathematician, philosopher and theologian Marin Mersenne (1588–1648) put forward a solution. He suggested an exponential system of tuning (i.e. one based on powers of numbers), where each note vibrates $\sqrt[12]{2}$ (= 1.059463094, or 1.06) times faster than the one before it. This divides the vibrations of any octave into 12 parts and, of course, ensures that the octave of any given note vibrates twice as quickly as the given note. In this way, each note of the keyboard is made to fit as well as possible into any scale. (Note that Mersenne's A was a lower pitch than our modern A.)

In round figures, the frequencies of vibration of the notes on Mersenne's system, starting with A440, are:

A	440	E	659.3
B♭	466.2	F	698.5
B	493.9	F#	740
C	523.3	G	784
C#	554.4	A♭	830.6
D	587.3	A'	880
E♭	622.3		

Common chords

Note that C# vibrates at 554 Hz – and in effect 440:554::4:5. Remembering our experience with the fifth (3:2), we are not surprised to find that the third gives another pleasing sound. Play A, C# and E together and you'll hear the common chord or triad (three notes – first, third and fifth) of A major. Table 5 shows the common chords of all the keys.

Table 5   Common chords (triads)

Key	Notes of common chord
C	C, E and G
G	G, B and D
D	D, F# and A
A	A, C# and E
E	E, G# and B
B	B, D# and F#
G♭ }	G♭, B♭ and D♭
F# }	F#, A# and C#
D♭	D♭, F and A♭
A♭	A♭, C and E♭
E♭	E♭, G and B♭
B♭	B♭, D and F
F	F, A and C

Note that the easiest way to fit these chords on the stave (in the key of C) is to think of sharps up to the halfway point (F#/G♭) and flats thereafter.

C   G   D   A   E   B   F# = G♭   D♭   A♭   E♭   B♭   F

Note that jazz tunes are more likely to be in keys towards the ends of the progression than in those towards the middle. Many bands play most tunes in F, B♭, sometimes E♭ and C and occasionally A♭ and G, but very often the original tune was not written in the key chosen. Tunes based on popular music of the 1920s and 1930s tend towards the C G D end, while those derived from marching bands tend towards the F B♭ E♭ end.

The circle of fifths

I have explained the interval of a fifth and its importance to tuning. The sequence of keys C G D A E B F#/G♭ D♭ A♭ E♭ B♭ F and back to C is called 'the circle of fifths' and it has another importance apart from tuning. If you take the common chords based on *any three consecutive notes in the circle*, you will find that they are the basis of hundreds and thousands of pieces of music – medieval, Renaissance, Baroque, Classical, Romantic, modern, folk tunes, popular melodies, all the traditional 8- and 12-bar blues, boogie-woogie, rock 'n' roll and the rest.

Given the key of a piece, its complementary keys are its subdominant (before it in the circle) and its dominant (after it in the circle). This use of three chords is so fundamental that it is known as the 'three-chord trick'.

The circle of fourths:

C up to G is the interval of a fifth; C' down to G is a fourth. If you read the sequence backwards, it's the circle of fourths.

A simple chord sequence

Let us look at this by example. In the diagram that follows, each box represents a bar of four beats.

Count 1 as you play the common chord of C and hold it for 2–3–4.

Count 1 as you play the common chord of F and hold it for 2–3–4.

Count 1 as you play the common chord of G and hold it for 2–3–4.

Count 1 as you play the common chord of C and hold it for 2–3–4.

Repeat that sequence. Congratulations! (Ugh!) You have just played an accompaniment to 'Little Brown Jug' in the key of C. Try it again, singing the melody.

Also note that F, C and G are consecutive notes in the circle of fifths; F and G are respectively the subdominant and dominant of the key of C. Moreover, the common chords of C, F and G use only white notes, so moving from one to another is very easy.

Further chord sequences

We now rewrite this chord sequence more conventionally in the way in which it might be found in a jazz musician's chord book:

C	F	G	C
C	F	G	C

So not only have you played a simple accompaniment; you have read a simple chord sequence. As I said before, most jazz musicians carry a chord book, with a chord sequence (such as our example) for each tune. This enables anyone unfamiliar with a given tune at least to accompany those who *do* know the tune. The brass and reeds probably do know the tune; all the other instrumentalists who can read the chords can join in to a greater or lesser effect according to their competence.

Let's just stay with 'Little Brown Jug': here it is in the key of F (consecutive notes from the circle of fifths B♭, F and C):

F	B♭	C	F
F	B♭	C	F

And here it is in B♭ (E♭ B♭ F from the circle of fifths):

B♭	E♭	F	B♭
B♭	E♭	F	B♭

Using the circle of fifths, you should now be able to write out and play the chord sequence for 'Little Brown Jug' in any key.

This is an extremely simple accompaniment; it consists in effect of the same four bars played over and over again. Most tunes are somewhat more complicated, but in jazz the principle of four beats to the bar is almost universal, as is the principle of bars grouped in fours.

Before we move on to look at some more complex tunes, we need to become familiar with some more complex chords.

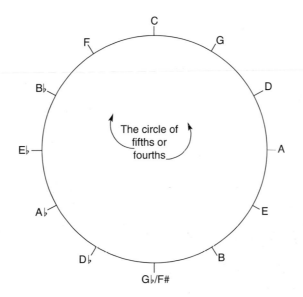

Further chords

In this chapter you will learn:

► *more about chords*
► *different types of scales*
► *about intervals.*

The minor scales

Learning the major scale and the major triads is a good start, as other chords can be thought of as modifications of their patterns. Of the minor scale, suffice it to say that:

1 The main characteristic from which it takes its name is that the third note is flattened: C, D, E♭, F ... instead of C, D, E, F ...

2 This gives us a set of *minor triads*, as shown in Table 6.

3 The key signature of a minor key is the same as that of the major key three semitones above it. Thus the key signature of A minor is the same as that of C major (which implies that you can play the scale of A minor on white notes only, starting on A). A minor is said to be the *relative minor* of C, a relationship to which we will refer when we look at some chord sequences.

Minor chords

To recap, a minor chord is a major chord with the third (i.e. the middle note of the triad) dropped a semitone.

Table 6   Minor chords

Key	Notes of common chord	Notes of minor chord	Written
C	C, E, G	C, E♭, G	Cm
G	G, B, D	G, B♭, D	Gm
D	D, F#, A	D, F, A	Dm
A	A, C#, E	A, C, E	Am
E	E, G#, B	E, G, B	Em
B	B, D#, F#	B, D, F#	Bm
F#⎫	F#, A#, C#	F#, A, C#	F#m
G♭⎭	G♭, B♭, D♭	F#, A, C#	G♭m
D♭	D♭, F, A♭	D♭, E, A♭	D♭m
A♭	A♭, C, E♭	A♭, B, E♭	A♭m
E♭	E♭, G, B♭	E♭, G♭, B♭	E♭m
B♭	B♭, D, F	B♭, D♭, F	B♭m
F	F, A, C	F, A♭, C	Fm

Again, we choose sharps and flats for ease of writing. It should be no surprise that the 'cross-over point' is now E minor, the relative minor of F#/G♭.

Cm Gm Dm Am Em Bm F#m D♭m A♭m E♭m B♭m Fm

The blues scale

Much is made of the so-called 'blue notes' which do not coincide with any of the notes of the chromatic scale (by which I mean that, if you state a key, its blue notes are not available on the piano, say – the blue notes are 'in the cracks').

The blues scale is better thought of 'coming down', since blues tunes always have a descending feeling (listen). So the blues scale in C:

C', B♭, G, F, E♭, D, C

Note that the 6th (A) is omitted. A 'funkier' version of the scale is:

C', B♭, G♭, F, E♭, D, C

Listen to the blues and assimilate its nuances.

Track 18

Seventh chords

Here's another confusion: when we speak of a 'seventh' in jazz, we really mean a flattened seventh. (If we mean a 'true' seventh, we say 'natural' or 'major seventh'.) The true seventh chord on C is C, E, G and B (written CΔ); the flattened or jazz seventh is C, E, G and B♭ (written C^7) (see Table 7).

Table 7 Seventh chords

Key	Notes of common chord	Notes of 7th chord	Written
C	C, E, G	C, E, G, B♭	C^7
G	G, B, D	G, B, D, F	G^7
D	D, F#, A	D, F#, A, C	D^7
A	A, C#, E	A, C#, E, G	A^7
E	E, G#, B	E, G#, B, D	E^7
B	B, D#, F#	B, D#, F#, A	B^7
G♭/F#	G♭, B♭, D♭	G♭, B♭, D♭, E	G♭^{7}/F#^{7}
D♭	D♭, F, A♭	D♭, F, A♭, B	D♭^{7}
A♭	A♭, C, E♭	A♭, C, E♭, G♭	A♭^{7}
E♭	E♭, G, B♭	E♭, G, B♭, D♭	E♭^{7}
B♭	B♭, D, F	B♭, D, F, A♭	B♭^{7}
F	F, A, C	F, A, C, E♭	F^7

C^7 G^7 D^7 A^7 E^7 B^7 F#^{7} D♭^{7} A♭^{7} E♭^{7} B♭^{7} F^7

You will find that the sound of the seventh chord – let's say C^7 – has an 'expectant' quality. The expectation is that the next chord is going to be an F major – F, A and C. The relationship is so important that the chord of C^7 with respect to the key of F is called the *dominant seventh* (see Table 4); that is to say, the seventh built on the dominant (perfect fifth) of the keynote, in this case F. We often find that the last chord of an *intro* (introduction) to a tune, or the last chord of a chorus preparing for the next chorus, is the dominant seventh.

If, instead of *resolving* the dominant seventh C^7 to F, we play F^7, this will lead in turn to B♭^{7}, E♭^{7} and so on. Continue in this way: you are playing backwards round the circle of fifths – round the circle of fourths, in fact.

As a means of practising chords and finding your way from one to the next, playing round the circle of fourths in *arpeggios* (notes of the chord played in rapid succession rather than simultaneously), C (major), C^7, F (major), F^7, B♭ … and so on, is a reasonably melodious exercise.

Sixth chords

The sixth has an ethereal quality; it is the common chord with the sixth note added:

C, E, (G), A (written C⁶). The fifth (G) is optional, according to the context in which the chord is played. Note that the notes of a sixth chord are the same as those of the relative minor of its key, but in a different order (an *inversion*) (see Table 8).

Table 8   Sixth chords

Key	Notes of common chord	Notes of 6th chord	Written
C	C, E, G	C, E, (G), A	C⁶
G	G, B, D	G, B, (D), E	G⁶
D	D, F#, A	D, F#, (A), B	D⁶
A	A, C#, E	A, C#, (E), F#	A⁶
E	E, G#, B	E, G#, (B), C#	E⁶
B	B, D#, F#	B, D#, (F#), G#	B⁶
G♭	G♭, B♭, D♭	G♭, B♭, (D♭), E♭	G♭⁶/F#⁶
D♭	D♭, F, A♭	D♭, F, (A♭), B♭	D♭⁶
A♭	A♭, C, E♭	A♭, C, (E♭), F	A♭⁶
E♭	E♭, G, B♭	E♭, G, (B♭), C	E♭⁶
B♭	B♭, D, F	B♭, D, (F), G	B♭⁶
F	F, A, C	F, A, C, D	F⁶

C⁶   G⁶   D⁶   A⁶   E⁶   B⁶F#⁶/G♭⁶D♭⁶   A♭⁶   E♭⁶   B♭⁶   F⁶

Diminished chords

I will now introduce another useful set of chords with a very simple pattern – the diminished chords. Play any note, leave out two notes and play the next, leave out two and play the next, leave out two and play the next, leave out two and play the next – which you will find is the octave of the note on which you started. So if you started on C, you played: C, E♭, G♭, A, C'. As you can see, this sequence would have been similar had you started on E♭, G♭ or A.

You might have started in two other places, playing:

D♭, E, G, B♭ ... or

D, F, A♭, B ...

Between them, these three diminished chords would have taken in all the notes of the keyboard. The diminished chord is written X° (see Table 9).

Table 9   The three diminished chords

C°	= E♭°	= G♭°	= A°
D♭°	= E°	= G°	= B♭°
D°	= F°	= A♭°	= B°

Another way of thinking of a diminished chord is as a minor triad with a flattened fifth and added sixth. I mention this because the idea of the 'shapes' of chords, and hence finger positions, is of great importance in being able to find the chord you want with the minimum of thought. So, for example, C major (C, G, E) moves easily to C#° (C#, E, G). You should make a habit of looking for such patterns.

Track 21

Augmented chords

The pattern of diminished chords 'works' because there are 12 semitones in the octave and we take every third note from our starting point. It will be no surprise to you by now that if we look at the effect of taking every fourth note from a starting point we arrive at another set of chords – the augmented chords, written X+. These may be thought of as major triads with their 5ths augmented and there are four (12 ÷ 3) different sequences (see Table 10).

Table 10 The four augmented chords

C+	= E+	= A♭+
D♭+	= F+	= A+
D+	= G♭+	= B♭+
E♭+	= G+	= B+

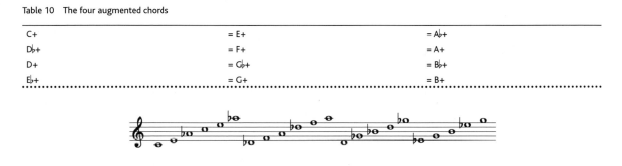

Track 22

Further intervals

To bring our survey to completion, I must mention a few further intervals which are, when you think about it, self-explanatory. C–C' (C' = C above) is an octave; C–D' is a 9th; C–E' is a 10th, C–F' is an 11th and so on. It will come as no surprise that you can have minor and augmented 9ths, 10ths, 11ths and so on. By the time you get to them, you should have no difficulty in working out what they mean.

With a full set of chords at our fingertips – the equivalent of X, Xm, X°, X+, X⁶' and X⁷ in all 12 keys – we have as much knowledge as we need to read the chords of any reasonable jazz tune.

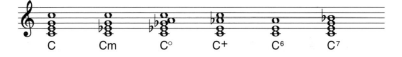

Track 23

Inversions

So far, I have presented chords as keynotes with a series of notes progressing upwards on them. However, there is no reason why the chosen notes should be played in that order – or, indeed, why they should all be present. For example, in context, a G and E played with the left hand and a G, B♭ and E played with the right hand is as much a chord of C⁷ – even without the C – as is C, E, G and B♭. A lot could be said about inversions, but conventional theoretical wisdom about them does not always sit easily with jazz practice. It is better to find out about what sounds better or worse by listening and practising.

Here are some inversions of the C⁷ chord:

🔊 **'CARELESS LOVE'**

Here are the chords and melody for a version of a traditional tune called 'Careless (or Loveless) Love'; try it:

The band plays on

How would the band play this? The higher-voiced front-line instruments would play the melody, or notes to harmonize with the melody, or something based on the melody. The lower-voiced front-line instruments might play the melody, or complete the three- (or more-) part harmony either closely with the other front-line instruments or providing strong *progressions* in the bass. The rhythm section would provide the rhythm (don't be surprised!), filling in the chordal structure; the guitar with full chords; and the piano would behave in a variety of ways depending on the pianist.

If you're playing this as a keyboard solo, work out a system – for instance, practise the melody line, then play the root note of each chord as an accompaniment; then the full chord on the first beat of each bar; then on each beat of the bar. It's bound to sound rather plonking at first, but as you begin to co-ordinate your hands and fingers you'll be able to transfer that mental and physical effort into listening to what you're playing and putting it into a more and more acceptable shape. Seated at your keyboard, you should be able to drive everyone mad as you work on this.

Oh, listen to the band

If you're listening to a recording, go over it several times, concentrating on a different instrument each time, listening both to what it's doing and how it fits in with the others. If you are able to persuade a band to play it for you, watch as well as listen to see how the musicians work with one another – or otherwise. This analytical approach to listening is hard work and, in the case of the live performance, may reveal the difference between *what* is played and the *environment* in which it is played. In other words (to paraphrase Sir Thomas again), you may think that it sounds better than it actually does.

Getting from A to B (and other letters)

Track 25

As you pursue your studies in jazz improvisation, you will find that in one sense 'playing a tune' is 'deciding how to get from one place to another'. In the bass of the 'Careless Love' example, the chord of the first bar is F, so it's a safe bet to play an F in your bass accompaniment. The chord of the second bar is C, so it's safe to play a C in your bass accompaniment and so on.

Looked at in another way: if beat 1 of bar 1 is F, you have beats 2, 3 and 4 of bar 1 to get to beat 1 of bar 2, which is C. So in bar 1 you could play F, E, D, D which would take you to C for bar 2. Bar 2 has to get you back to F (via C⁷), which could be achieved as C, B, A, G, bringing us back to an F. Treat bars 3 and 4 similarly:

Listen to the bass parts or instruments in a jazz ensemble and you'll hear what I mean.

If you wish to continue to develop your playing – and I hope you will – I must at this stage leave you to practise and listen and practise some more. I will next turn to a selection of types of jazz and tell you about some of the basic chord sequences.

19

Chord sequences

In this chapter you will learn:

▶ *to recognize and play different types of chord sequence*

▶ *about interpretation.*

Introduction

We now move on to study some chord sequences. First, we will look at some 'building blocks' – groups of chords which crop up time and again – and then embark on complete tunes. When you become familiar with the building blocks you'll be able to put them together in different ways as required by different tunes. The principle of Mozart's waltz generator is not entirely frivolous.

One thing I should stress at the outset is that there is not necessarily one definitive sequence for any given tune – it can be a matter of interpretation. The chords written on the sheet music may not necessarily be the best ones to play. The only bad chords are the ones that don't fit what you're doing.

Note that my examples are all written in four- or eight-bar phrases. You should get into the habit of writing your chord sequences in that way – it helps you to see at a glance any phrases or sequences there are in a tune and also helps you to keep track of where you are when you are playing.

Rather than load too many new problems on you, I have used a fairly limited range of keys. You should be able to *transpose* any piece into any key you wish – I leave it to you.

The symbol % means that a bar is the same as the one that precedes it. However, if bar 5 is the same as bar 4 we write the chord symbol rather than % – it helps to preserve the four-bar groups.

A bar with two chords in it means two beats of each of the two chords. If there are more than two chords in a bar, dots above indicate how many beats of each. Chords in square brackets [X] in a bar indicate an alternative.

'Calypso' sequence

What trumpeter Owen Bryce dubbed the calypso sequence moves from the tonic to its dominant seventh and back, a sequence on which countless calypsos have been built. It is a very easy 'amen' sort of cadence. It occurs in numerous tunes, jazz and otherwise; think of the beginning of 'The Liberty Bell' (of *Monty Python* fame) for example:

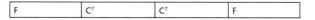

F	C⁷	C⁷	F

'Final' sequence

An often used final sequence, i.e. one that rounds off a chorus, can be simply rendered:

F F⁷	B♭ B♭m	F C⁷	F	(a)

There are many other ways of achieving a chorus ending, for example:

F F⁷	B♭ F°	F D⁷	D♭ C⁷ F	(b)

Put the calypso together with a final sequence for a complete tune:

F	C⁷	C⁷	F	(c)
F F⁷	B♭ B♭m	F Dm	G⁷ C⁷ F	

The following sequence is found in many tunes and was an ODJB favourite. It is the main theme of such tunes as 'Tiger Rag', *Won't You Come Home, Bill Bailey?*, 'Fidgetty Feet' and others:

F	✗	✗	✗	F	✗	C⁷	✗
C⁷	✗	✗	✗	C⁷	✗	F	✗
F	✗	✗	✗	F⁷	✗	B♭	✗
B♭	B°	F	D⁷	G⁷	C⁷	F	✗

Track 29

'High Society'

Now I'm going to take you through the chords for an old New Orleans marching tune with an intro, two strains (or themes), a bridge and a main strain with an interlude. The tune is in the key of B♭, starting on the dominant seventh (F⁷). It begins with a four-bar *intro* (introduction):

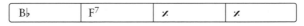

B♭	F⁷	✗	✗

The first strain comprises an eight-bar calypso sequence starting and finishing on the dominant seventh and an eight-bar sequence incorporating Gm (the relative minor of B♭):

F⁷	F⁷	B♭	✗	F⁷	✗	B♭	✗
Gm	✗	D⁷	Gm	Gm	✗	C⁷	F⁷

This strain is repeated (2 × 16 bars) and the tune then moves to the brighter second strain (brighter because it doesn't have the minor chords), another 16-bar sequence in which the second eight bars incorporate the final sequence. It finishes on the keynote rather than leaving us hanging on the dominant seventh as did the first strain:

F⁷	✗	B♭	✗	C⁷	✗	F⁷	✗
B♭	D⁷	E♭	E°	B♭	F⁷	B♭	✗

This is also repeated (2 × 16 bars). We will not be hearing either of those two strains again; the signal that we've reached the end of that section of the piece and are about to start another is a four-bar bridge passage to take us from the introductory key of B♭ to the main key of E♭ (B♭ now appearing as the dominant seventh):

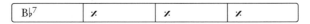

B♭⁷	✗	✗	✗

This bridge is followed by the 32-bar march chorus played *ensemble* (all together) except for the last two bars of the second eight, where the line across the top indicates a *break*; everyone stops playing except for a chosen instrument, which plays a couple of bars in B♭ ad lib:

E♭	✗	✗	✗	E♭	E♭ A♭	E♭	✗
B♭⁷	✗	E♭	✗	F⁷	✗	B♭⁷	✗
E♭	✗	✗	✗	E♭	E♭ A♭	E♭	E♭⁷
A♭	A°	E♭	C⁷	F⁷	B♭⁷	E♭	✗

Note that the first eight bars and the third eight bars of this chorus are of the 'Bill Bailey' type and almost the same, except at the end of the third eight bars where the dominant seventh (E♭⁷) prepares us for the following A♭.

Ensemble

In other musical forms, the Italian word *tutti* is used to indicate that everyone plays, while the French word *ensemble* refers to the collection of musicians. In jazz, the word *ensemble* is used for everyone playing together – presumably it is the French influence from New Orleans.

The second eight bars of this chorus are analogous to the first eight bars of the second strain, but transposed up a fourth (F to B♭). Similarly, the last eight bars of this chorus are analogous to the last eight bars of the second strain (the final sequence), again transposed up a fifth (B♭ to E♭).

After the ensemble chorus comes an eight-bar interlude passage in C minor (the relative minor of E♭). This interlude ends on the dominant seventh (B♭⁷) to lead into the E♭ chorus again:

| Cm | ✗ | G⁷ | ✗ | Cm | ✗ | G⁷ | ✗ |
| Fm | ✗ | Cm | ✗ | A♭⁷ | ✗ | G⁷ | B♭⁷ |

As I said, the chorus was played ensemble first time around; after the interlude, by tradition, the clarinet plays a featured solo first framed by the New Orleans clarinettist Alphonse Picou. Picou adapted his solo from piccolo 'trio' practice; you may be able to recall the piccolo trio in the Sousa march 'Stars and Stripes for Ever' ('Be kind to your web-footed friends').

The chorus

The main part of any complete tune is the chorus. In ballads, this is contrasted with the verse, an introductory strain which is often forgotten in favour of the chorus it once introduced (indeed, an interesting game is to play a verse and see if anyone knows what chorus follows it). Here, I'm following usual parlance and referring to the main tune which is played many times, in contrast to the 'strains' which appear only at the start.

After the trio, we have a repeat of the interlude and then as many choruses as the leader of the band thinks are necessary to give a solo to everyone who wants one. For variety, the break (at the end of the second eight) might be given to a different instrument from that playing the solo; the second instrument would then carry on to the next break before handing over.

The trio

Trio is a word derived from the seventeenth-century composition pattern when one strain played twice sandwiches a second, contrasting, strain (A–B–A). The B strain was initially a harmony played on three wind instruments, hence the word 'trio'; it is also (in that form) one of three movements.

The practice was carried forward to march composition, and marches are well known for a rousing A strain to start and finish sandwiching a quieter and more thoughtful B strain, sometimes in a different key.

One of the best-known trios is the strain known as 'Land of Hope and Glory' in Elgar's Pomp and Circumstance March No. 1 in D.

The leader of the band may decide to play another interlude before the final (rousing) chorus, and the last eight bars might be repeated as an *outro* (the opposite of an intro).

If you become familiar with that fairly lengthy analysis of 'High Society' and follow it as you listen to a band playing it, you will be able to appreciate the way the parts of the performance fit together.

Three-chord circular sequence

Track 30

This starts on the subdominant, followed by the tonic and then the dominant seventh. The fourth bar ends on the seventh of the keynote to lead us back to the subdominant again, and round and round it goes (key F):

Notes to accompany the recordings

Keith Nichols is considered to be one of the foremost authorities on classic jazz and ragtime, specializing in all the older piano styles including those of Scott Joplin, Jelly Roll Morton, James P Johnson, Duke Ellington and Fats Waller.

Born in 1945, Keith took his first music lessons on piano and accordion at the age of five; at 15, he became Great Britain Junior Champion Accordionist. He turned professional after graduating from the Guildhall School of Music, touring with the jazz-comedy band Levity Lancers in which he played piano, trombone and tuba.

Keith first visited the United States in 1976 as a member of Richard Sudhalter's New Paul Whiteman Orchestra, appearing in Philadelphia and at Carnegie Hall, New York. His recording credits include three solo albums for EMI and a host of others for Decca, including one with Bing Crosby. Since the mid-1980s he has been featured on more than 20 albums for the American Stomp Off label, both as sideman and bandleader.

In 1977 he formed the Midnite Follies Orchestra with arranger Alan Cohen, and has written many arrangements and transcriptions in the style of the 1920s and 1930s, notably for the New York Jazz Repertory Company, the Smithsonian Institution Masterworks series and the Pasadena Roof Orchestra.

In 1990 Keith was invited by musical director Bob Wilber to play the piano part of Hoagy Carmichael on the soundtrack of the feature film *Bix*, recorded in Rome.

He continues to record and perform prolifically in the UK, the United States and in many other countries. He lectures on and demonstrates the history of jazz at the Royal Academy of Music and Trinity College of Music, where he recently recreated the 1924 Paul Whiteman concert *Experiment in Modern Music*, which included a performance of *Rapsody in Blue* with the original instrumentation. Other recreations have included Benny Goodman's 1938 Carnegie Hall concert, with the Royal Academy Big Band. His latest orchestral venture was the formation of the ten-piece Blue Devils to perform music of the 1920s, 1930s and 1940s.

Throughout his career, Keith Nichols has given solo and small-group concerts, promoting the interest and excitement of ragtime and jazz according to the old masters. He was thus an obvious choice to 'get inside' the feeling of what was needed to illustrate the development of jazz, and composed the eight tracks specially for this *Teach Yourself* title.

With **Keith Nichols** you will hear trumpeter **Rico Tomasso**, one of Britain's brightest and most versatile jazz stars. Coming from a family of jazz musicians, Rico spent 12 years with the Pasadena Roof Orchestra, and has worked with Keith on many special projects. He now performs regularly with Ray Gelato.

The versatile reedsman you hear on clarinet and tenor is **James Evans**, another enthusiast for demonstrating styles of the past from the sound of George Lewis to post bebop. James has played with the New Orleans-style bands of Phil Mason and Max Collie, and is currently featured in a very entertaining group The Boston Tea Party.

Track 1: 'French Quarter Parade' is in Classic New Orleans style, featuring a funereal introduction moving into a brisk stomp with piano in the tradition of Jelly Roll Morton (trumpet, clarinet, piano).

Track 2: 'Bix Trix' is set in the tradition of the popular white jazz of the twenties. It echoes the sound of Bix Beiderbecke and Red Nichols (trumpet, alto, piano).

Track 3: 'South Side Chicago Blues' is in the style of the 'Race' blues of the early twenties (trumpet, clarinet, piano).

Track 4: 'Stridin' in Harlem' is a piano solo demonstrating the difficult 'stride' style perfected by James P Johnson, which found a wide audience with the popularity of Fats Waller in the thirties (piano solo).

Track 5: 'A Purple Mist' is a slow dreamy piece in the style of Duke Ellington (trumpet, clarinet/alto, piano).

Track 6: 'Young Satchmo' is a trumpet and piano duet, as performed by Louis Armstrong during his formative years in Chicago in the 1920s (trumpet, piano).

Track 7: 'Boogie-Woogie Cocktail' is a solo demonstration of the boogie-woogie styles of Pine-top Smith and Pete Johnson (piano solo).

Track 8: 'Swing with Benny' is a piano and clarinet duet typical of the chamber music swing of the late 1930s, Benny Goodman style (clarinet, piano).

Bb7	℅	F	℅
C7	℅	F	F7

Examples of this sequence ad nauseam are 'Bucket's Got a Hole in It' and 'Girls Go Crazy about the Way I Walk'.

Four-chord circular sequence

This starts on a dominant seventh and then follows the circle of fourths (key F):

D7	℅	G7	℅
C7	℅	F	℅

Examples of tunes containing this sequence are 'Up a Lazy River' and 'Ballin' the Jack'.

Track 31 **'UP A LAZY RIVER'**

D7	℅	G7	℅
C7	℅	F	℅
D7	℅	G7	℅
Bb7 F°	F D7	G7 C7	G7 C7

G7 C7	F

Each chorus has a two bar *tag*, or *double ending*:

Track 32 **'DITTY FOR KEITH'**

The four-chord circular sequence does not necessarily have to start on the dominant 7th; in 'Ditty for Keith' for example (key F):

F E	Eb D	G C7	F C+
F E	Eb D	C G	CC° CC+
F	A7	Dm	F°
F E	Eb D	G C	F

Track 33 ## A ragtime sequence

I assembled the following five strains (here in Bb) as a demonstration of how ragtime works.

Ragtime pieces normally have four strains at the most, but this shows the elements from which to choose – for example A–A–B–B–A–C–bridge–D–D.

The intro uses the dominant seventh:

F7	℅	℅	℅

The first strain (played twice) is a straightforward echo of march practice:

Bb	Bb Bb7	Eb E°	Bb	Bb	℅	C7	F7
Bb	Bb Bb7	Eb E°	D7	Eb E°	Bb G7	C7 F7	Bb

The second strain (played twice) starts on the dominant seventh:

F⁷	✗	B♭	✗	F⁷	✗	B♭°	✗
F⁷	✗	B♭	B♭⁷	E♭ E°	B♭ G⁷	C⁷ F⁷	B♭

The third strain (played twice) starts on the subdominant with a three-chord circular sequence:

E♭	✗	B♭	✗	F⁷	✗	B♭	B♭⁷
E♭	✗	B♭	B♭⁷	E♭ E°	B♭ G⁷	C⁷ F⁷	B♭

The fourth strain (played twice) is based on the four-chord circular sequence:

G⁷	✗	C⁷	✗	F⁷	✗	B♭	✗
G⁷	✗	C⁷	✗	F⁷	✗	B♭	✗

The fifth strain is played once to round the piece off:

B♭	F⁷	B♭	F⁷	B♭	Gm	C⁷	F⁷
B♭	F⁷	B♭	F⁷	B♭ B♭⁷	E♭ E°	B♭ F⁷	B♭

'The Entertainer'

Let us now look at that well-known tune by Scott Joplin, 'The Entertainer'. It is worthwhile comparing its development with that of 'High Society'. 'The Entertainer' is in C, so the intro is in the dominant G⁷:

G⁷	✗	✗	✗

The first strain is played twice:

C C⁷	F Fm	C G⁷	C	C C⁷	F	D⁷	G⁷
C C⁷	F Fm	C G⁷	C	C C⁷	F Fm	C G⁷	C [C G⁷]

The second strain is also played twice:

C	C C⁷	F Fm	C	C	✗	D⁷	G⁷
C	C C⁷	F Fm	C C⁷	F C°	C A⁷	D⁷ G⁷	C

The first strain is then repeated once; then without further ado comes the third strain, in the (subdominant) key of F, which is played twice:

F	B♭	Dm	Gm	Gm F	F Dm	E⁷	Am C⁷
F	B♭	Dm	Gm	Gm F	F D⁷	G⁷ C⁷	F

A short bridge passage between the third and fourth strains:

F	C°	C	A⁷	D⁷	G⁷	C

takes us into the final strain in C (the key in which the piece opened) which ought to start on the dominant seventh (G⁷), but in fact starts on the subdominant (F):

F	✗	C	✗	G⁷	✗	C°	C
G⁷	✗	C	C⁷	F	C A⁷	D⁷ G⁷	C

The blues

EIGHT-BAR BLUES

The earliest blues were of the eight-bar form:

Intro chorus			
F	F⁷	B♭	✗
F	C⁷	F	F C⁷ How

First verse			
F long, how	F⁷ long has that	B♭ ev' nin' train been	✗ gone? Lord, how
F long, how	C long? Lordy, how	F long?	F

Jimmy Yancey's (wordless) 'How Long Blues' is an example of this form.

16-BAR BLUES

The choruses of the eight-bar blues tend to want to go in pairs, so forming the (still primitive) 16-bar blues:

F	F⁷	B♭	✗
F	C⁷	F	F C⁷
F	F⁷	B♭	✗
F	C⁷	F	✗

'Trouble in Mind' is an example of this form.

12-BAR BLUES

By far the most common blues form is the 12-bar (in B). Whatever else you can play or can't play, the one thing you *must* be able to play is a 12-bar blues in B:

B♭	✗	✗	B♭⁷
E♭	✗	B♭	✗
F⁷	✗	B♭	B♭ F⁷ 1

B♭ walked all night with my	✗ 32–20 in my	✗ han' § – – –	B♭⁷ § – – Yes, I
E♭ walked all night with my	✗ 32–20 in my	B♭ han' § – – –	✗ § – – –
F⁷ Lookin' for my woman;	✗ well, she gone off with	B♭ another man § –	B♭ F⁷ § – – –

In this form, the first line is repeated to allow the singer (so it is said) to devise the second line (A–A–B). As I said earlier, the blues lyric has to be sung for it to stand up to strict poetic scrutiny. The § – symbol indicates the instrumental *fill-in* at the end of the line; the interplay between voice and accompaniment is another essential part of the whole. If you haven't yet done so, I urge you to listen to an earthy blues record and hear what I'm talking about.

Having stated the basic blues sequence, we can look at some of the many variations. First, extra subdominant chords:

B♭	E♭	B♭	B♭⁷
E♭	E♭[m]	B♭	✗
F⁷	E♭	B♭ E♭	B♭

Extra variety by the use of the so-called Dixieland ending (spoken of as 'going down to G'):

B♭	E♭	B♭	B♭⁷
E♭	✗	B♭ [E♭ D⁷]	G⁷
C⁷	F⁷	B♭	✗

One exercise of interest is to compile as many plausible 12-bar blues sequences – using particularly the tonic, subdominant and dominant chords – as you can.

The 32-bar ballad form

Track 34

Let us now look at a country and western type of song: 'When You and I Were Young, Maggie'. It follows the same A–A–B–A pattern as countless other songs. The first eight bars give us a good idea of what the tune will be like:

In bar 2, the F⁷ dominant leads to the B♭ of bar 3.

In bar 4, B♭ is OK and so would B♭m be, but F° is a more exciting transitional chord.

In bar 6, F would do, but moving to C⁷ via D⁷ and G⁷ is more exciting.

The second eight bars repeat and complete the phrase of the first eight:

Now we come to the *middle eight* (which obviously isn't in the middle, but that's what it's always called) which provides a contrasting tune:

This ends in such a way that we're ready to return to a repeat of the second eight to finish the sequence:

In bar 4, B♭ is OK and so would B♭m be, but F° is a more exciting transitional chord.

The A–A–B–A pattern is one of the most common; the chord sequence of the middle eight often departs further from the A sequence than it does in 'Maggie'.

'ROSETTA'

The first eight:

| F | C+ | F | D⁷ | G⁷ | C⁷ | F | C⁷ | ∕ |

As before, the second eight repeats and completes the phrase of the first eight:

| F | C+ | F | D⁷ | G⁷ | C⁷ | F | ∕ |

Here, the middle eight provides a more contrasting tune than in the previous example:

| Am | E⁷ | Am | Fm | C | G | C | C+ |

As before, a repeat of the second eight finishes the sequence:

| F | C+ | F | D⁷ | G⁷ | C⁷ | F | ∕ |

Stride piano

The word *stride* is applied to a piano technique where the left hand plays a bass note (or octave, or 10th or even 12th) on the first beat of the bar, followed by a chord further up the keyboard on the second beat and variations thereon.

Listen to masters of stride playing, such as James P Johnson and Fats Waller for a practical demonstration of the technique.

Boogie-woogie

This form always follows a 12-bar blues sequence, often in the key of G:

G	∕	∕	G⁷
C	∕	G	∕
D⁷	∕ [C⁷]	G	∕

or C:

C	∕.	∕.	C⁷
F	∕.	C	∕.
G	∕. [F]	C	∕.

The characteristic of boogie is the eight-to-the-bar bass figure, repeated (often with little modification) in the tonic, subdominant and dominant. While the left hand is busy laying down a solid rhythm, the right hand states an idea in the first bar or two of the chorus and develops it.

In the following examples, I will give one bar of each of the three keys; you must assemble the elements in the right order.

Here is the well-known 'walking bass' in C, F and G:

And another well-known form ('Pinetop's Blues' – F, B♭ and C):

And Meade Lux Lewis's 'Honky Tonk Train Blues' (G, D and C)

Finally, a bass figure often used by that popular pianist of the 1950s, Winifred Atwell:

Conclusion

The foregoing explanations and examples will have enabled you to appreciate something of the structure of jazz, either as a listener or as a player – especially a keyboard player. I hope that you have understood and enjoyed our journey through the history and development of the music, that I have helped you to get from it at least as much as you hoped to, and that I have inspired you to continue with a new interest as a listener or player.